CHOOSING SURVIVAL

How I Endured a Brutal Attack and a Lifetime of Trauma through the Power of Action, Choice, and Self Expression

LYNN F FORN

Choosing Survival

How I Endured a Brutal Attack and a Lifetime of Trauma through the Power of Action, Choice, and Self Expression

Lynn F Forney

ISBN Paperback: 979-8-9861831-0-7

Disclaimer

This memoir depicts actual events in the life of the author as truthfully as recollection permits. Others involved may have a different impression, recollection, or perspective of the events portrayed. Conversations in this book are not exact quotes but reconstructed to the best of the author's memory. When possible, the author presents third-party resources to reinforce the events presented within.

To be clear, David M. was not formally tried or charged with the attack on Lynn Forney. As indicated in news articles, including the one cited in this book, he remains a suspect and is serving time for similar crimes.

The information in this book is not intended to diagnose, treat, cure, or prevent any condition or disease. Please seek advice from your healthcare provider for your personal health concerns before taking any advice from this book. The author and publisher assume no responsibility.

Interior and Cover Design: STOKE Publishing
Author Photo Credit: Laura Flannery
https://www.lauraflannerystudio.com/

Praise for Choosing Survival

The writing is accessible and honest, often providing examples of personal growth through the raw power inherent in the underlying story. Lynn's voyage is an emotional tour de force, bringing the reader easily from a painful, dark past to the value of vulnerability explored in similar fashion to Brene Brown, and ending in emotional enlightenment, complete with tools and suggestions for the personal improvement of any audience. By page 14 I had formulated a list of people in my life that need to read this book, by 21 it included me, and at 49 it was clear everyone can benefit from this story. Initially I requested permission to let my other half help with the evaluation of the book; she is on the "page 14 list" and will read it independently, as I have completed the book and review before she has started – I could not put it down once I began reading.

— Manuel Mora Teaching and Learning
Coordinator, Social Sciences Dept.
Davenport University.

This is a story that needed to be told. I salute Lynn's courage in sharing her quest for closure and hope it inspires other women to not give up on their own healing journeys. The author's determination to find healing and peace after devastating trauma is a testament to an unbreakable, resilient spirit.

—Joan Bardo, DNP, CNM.

It's a roller-coaster ride from start to finish, told in a conversational, nonlinear fashion that, at times, creates a sense of nervousness on the page which directly translates into reader engagement at a primal and emotional level. Forney's writing is brisk, irreverent, funny.

Her ability to find hope on the path of her own life gives her a greater sense of empathy and sympathy for others finding themselves on their own twisted trail, In the end, she offers her readers a light in the darkness ... It's a journey worth taking. Just make sure to hang on tight!

— Christian Hokenson, Author and Screenwriter

This awe-inspiring book captures the reader's attention from beginning to end, and offers a unique perspective of society's response to trauma while also validating individuals' experiences. It is a book for those who have experienced trauma and those who would like insight into the lifelong journey of overcoming physical, mental, and emotional wounds. By courageously sharing her personal story with the world, Lynn gives space for her audience to open up about their own traumas and continue on their path of healing. I loved every moment.

— April Mackey

Choosing Survival by Lynn F. Forney is an evocative, authentic, harrowing, and heart wrenching testimony of trauma, recovery and inner strength. Forney gives the reader a vivid, intimate glimpse into her personal experiences with darkness, shining a light on that darkness by telling her story. Through a combination of poetry and prose, I found myself deeply moved, brought to tears, and inspired to action by the author's words.

— Kellis McSparrin Oldenburg, Assistant Professor of Dance at Belhaven University

Lynn has shown exceptional bravery in telling her story. She felt alone, but because she didn't hit the delete button, now no one else has to feel isolated in the pain of their trauma or the struggle with their mental health. If everyone shared their experiences with such honesty and candor, the world would be a better place. It would be a more nurturing environment where victims and those struggling with depression and anxiety would not feel like they have to hide or have to fight to be heard and believed, but the perpetrators would be the ones ostracized and oppressed. I'm so glad she fought for healing in her life and that she used her pain to be a creative rather than a destructive force in this world. I'm so proud to call her my friend. Enough Talk!

— Casey Heflin

Choosing Survival is a candid account of one woman's harrowing experience, and the unexpected emotional journey that followed. Lynn Forney has painted a vivid and honest portrait of her lifelong struggle with depression and PTSD, and her personal fight to find happiness and healing through therapy and dance.

— Sherri Eakin Sande

Contents

To my husband, Lucas Pettey. I love you so much. You support me in ways I can't even fully understand, and for that, I'm eternally grateful. I know that we've traversed some rocky terrain (and I'm sorry when I've been the cause), but I know we are stronger together. You give me the freedom to be myself, and the patience I need when I'm still figuring out what that means. You are insanely intelligent, talented, funny, and kind. I'm happy we are on this journey together and can't wait to see what's next for us. I love you more than I love roller coasters! (And that's saying a lot!). Thank you for loving me.

To all survivors. Especially those of David M.

Chapter 1

I can't even breathe

I begin to feel my eyelids flutter. Slowly. Gently at first. I feel so groggy, unsure of where I am. As my eyelids begin to blink open, only a tiny amount, I hear a voice.

"She's starting to wake up. Look."

A few quiet gasps follow. I begin to see figures around me. Staring. Tense. Nothing more than silhouettes. Confusion wraps around my brain. Foggy. Muddy. Where am I? I continue to peer through the murkiness, adjusting to the light. Suddenly, it's as if the tip of a tornado touches down on top of my head. Swiftly pulling any grogginess from my body up into its fierce cyclone. My eyes rapidly pop open. Alert. Wide. Panicked.

As panic shoots through me, I can see the figures clearly now. "Her eyes are open." Murmurs follow with bated breaths. I feel my lips pressed around a hard plastic tube. My throat is stuffed full. I feel like I'm suffocating. I want to scream out, "I can't breathe! I can't breathe!" But I am unable to form words. I am unable to cry out. I am unable to even create a breath.

I feel like I'm dying. I try to put my hand up to my throat. Desperate to ask for help. To communicate what I'm feeling. I can't breathe! I can't breathe! Someone help me! Please! I pull and pull and pull, but I'm unable to move my hand. It feels so heavy. Glued to the bed. Pinned down under a force I can not fight. I try desperately to lift my arm. It won't budge. Lift. Lift. Lift. I try to will it with all my might. I'm terrified. Why can't I move?? I quickly realize my entire body is being held captive by the same force that has trapped my arm. My eyes are wild with fear. Why won't any of you help me?

My terror builds as I'm unable to ask for help. Everyone around me stays still. Staring. Looking at me like I'm on display. God, what is happening to me? Everything inside of me is screaming out. But I can do nothing. I can't even breathe. Despite this intense fear coursing through my veins, my eyelids begin to descend. The heaviness of my body begins to seep into them. No, no, no. I need help! I struggle against them. Stay open, I plead. But they do not listen. I feel my eyes roll back. My eyelids flutter. My vision begins to blur. The edges get fuzzy. I try to fight. I need help! Please! But no words can escape my mouth that is still stuffed full. The tornado returns and as it touches down, exhaustion seeps into my head. My body quickly drinks it up. The voice in my head becomes more distant. Hollow. I can no longer fight. My eyelids continue to flutter. My vision continues to fade. Until, once again, it is dark.

Chapter 2

Fall 1997

A simple conversation can change your life.

"Hey, Ric, what do you think about me changing my major to dance?" I asked.

His eyebrows lifted as his spine grew a bit taller, and replied, "Well...I think that's a wonderful idea."

"Okay," I replied with a nod, "Done."

I grew up mainly in Boca Raton, Florida. I attended Dreyfoos School of the Arts from eighth through twelfth grade as a dance major. I also danced with Boca Ballet Theatre Company since its inception the same year I started Arts School. The summer before my senior year of high school, I lived in New York City for two months to study at the Alvin Ailey School of Dance. To say that dance was (and still is) a huge part of my life would be an understatement. I also felt strongly about academics. I graduated in the top ten of my class, and I wanted to attend a "good school" when it came to college. Looking back, a part of me wishes I had moved back to NYC after high school, but at the time, I felt that getting a college degree was extremely important and non-negotiable. And, honestly, I can't imagine not working with, and being mentored by, the incredible teachers and students I had the privilege to study with while there. I seldom say I'm proud of myself for anything, but I'm very proud of my BFA with Highest Honors from the University of Florida.

That moment with my professor was a huge turning point for me. I had planned on getting a "practical degree" while continuing to study dance. I was so excited to start college. A new chapter. My best friends from high school were attending UF as well, so it made it that much sweeter. I had many fun times during my first year of school. But I was met with many dark ones as well. I had struggled with depression since childhood, and I was incredibly hard on myself. My perfectionism had no limits. I'm not sure I can really pinpoint why everything caught up to me so fiercely my freshman year, but it did. I crashed. I needed help. Even though it felt like a huge setback, I decided to take my sophomore year off from school and live at home. I spent a lot of time in therapy. I thought it helped. And, to an extent, it did.

I returned to school in the fall excited. Hopeful. Joyful. Focusing on my studies. Being with my friends again. Positive I was in a much better place. When I packed up to move back to school, I failed to notice I had a stowaway. Depression had tucked itself into a dark corner of my suitcase. Burrowing itself deep. Staying out of sight. Hiding in the shadows. At first, I was blissfully unaware of its presence. But depression is sneaky, stealthy, and patient. Slowly, steadily, it seeped back into my body, taking over me once more.

Not again. I could not succumb to this again. As it became harder and harder to get out of bed every day, my frustration grew. There had to be a different solution. I didn't want to leave college again, but I couldn't continue this way. But what else could I do?

That conversation with my professor was rather impulsive. I don't recall much thought about changing my major to dance before that day. I certainly didn't make a list of pros and cons, or what future jobs I could get. I remember it vividly, however, and it changed the course of my college career, as well as my life. UF has had new facilities since I was a student, but at the time, our dance studio was in the same building as the basketball arena. It was nicknamed "The Cage" because it had a large blue chain linked fence around it. Outside the studio was a large walkway, and there were a lot of plants along the edge that were separated by a short concrete wall you could sit on. Ric was sitting there, waiting for the current class to end. His jazz class was next. I was standing next to him. A few moments of silence passed, and I asked if I should become a dance major. Suddenly. Spontaneously. Instinctively. His response was all I needed to say yes and make that change.

Slowly, day by day, the depression that consumed my

body began to flow out of me. Small droplets trickled out at first. Then it opened to a small but steady stream. As the darkness left, the light filled the empty space it left behind. I felt like a huge weight had been lifted off my shoulders. This was where I belonged. This made me feel purposeful. This lit the flame that ignited my soul.

Chapter 3

I was five. He was eight

My body feels heavy as I hang my head. My chest sinks, pulling my heart down with it. The leaves are brown and crispy at my feet, dancing ever so slightly in the soft breeze.

"No," I say softly. I don't like it when he asks this of me. I don't want to do that. I don't like it.

"Pleeeease," he begs. I bring my eyes back to his. Vivid blue. Wide. Pleading. Desperate. The bright blue sky stretches out behind him. Radiant beams of sun descend upon us. His blond hair twinkles as each strand finds its light.

"No," I say again as I shake my head. My eyebrows furrow as I gaze upon the leaves once more, still twirling in their soft ballet.

"Come on, no one's looking," he reasons. All I can do is gently shake my head from side to side as my chest burrows itself deeper. Why is he making me do this again? I don't like it. I said no. Why does he keep asking and asking?

He continues to insist. "No one's going to see. Come on. Just do it. We'll do it together on the count of three. One." I briefly look at him. His hands are grasping the waist of his pants. His body is directly facing mine. My body is facing the back side of my house, sideways to his. "Two." I look at the long beams of siding that stretch across the wall. A soft yellow color. Beginning to show their age. Dread washes over me as I grab my pants. Robotically. Obediently. "Three." I pull my pants down and squat. Mirroring him. He stares at my body. A large grin stretches across his face. His eyebrows raise high. His eyes transfixed on my private parts. Private. That's what they're supposed to be. But he always wants them to be on display. A show. A spectacle. For his pleasure.

The Cage

I thought I was done with this place
Yet, here I am again
Over and over you've seduced me
When will I just give in?

I've clawed my way out so many times
Fingertips bleeding and raw
Why must I keep fighting to stay above ground
When I'm destined to relapse and fall.

Your iron bars are strong and thick
Oozing with sludge and decay
This thick substance moves fluidly
Engulfing all that are in its way.

I feel the dark substance tickle my feet
As I lay, curled up on your floor
Unsure how you found me again
And drew me back in for more.

I look up, through the cage you've trapped me in
And see how far beneath the earth we are
The air is thick and moist
Smelling of sulfur and tar.

The sludge continues up my toes
Wrapping around my feet
Slithering around my legs
As I lay motionless in defeat.

Small butterflies of light dance
Flickering in the darkness around me
Alas, I realize those are bits of my strength
Peeling off my motionless body.

I want to escape, scream and thrash
How could you do this to me again
I grab the bars to pull myself up
But your darkness is closing in.

You have no face, yet I know your smile
That sinister Cheshire Cat grin
You can't bear to leave me alone for long
You refuse to let me win.

I'm exhausted, lost, and scared
Begging for this to end
How many times can I escape?
How do I find the fortitude to ascend?

The black substance continues to envelop me
I plead for my strength to return
I look up once more to see a sliver of light
Is this the hope for which I yearn?

I reach through the thick iron bars
Dripping with dark delight
I know all too well your deceitful promises
So I pull with all my might.

The sludge senses this desperation in me
This urgency to escape once more
It tightens and thickens with disdain
And whispers you are what I adore.

Your grasp is all encompassing
I don't know how much more I can fight
I fear I'll never leave this cage
But I also fear that I might.

Chapter 4

"God, if you really love me, you won't make me wake up tomorrow."

At one point in my life, this was my nightly prayer. It's difficult to think back to this time and even more difficult to admit it. Depression (ie, The Cage) is an ugly, treacherous beast. Years ago, I was told by a group therapist that using the term depression to describe general feelings of sadness and the like was incorrect. I recently relayed this to a couple of friends. I was quickly met with, "that's not really accurate" from one of them, even though they have struggled with it themselves. The conversation quickly went elsewhere, and I just sank. On my little boat. Out in the middle of the ocean. Feeling, like so many other times in my life, unheard and unimportant. Although depression may be grammatically correct to describe a "depressed mood", I can understand the importance of distinguishing the two.

Sadness, grief, melancholy, heartbreak, loss. The list can certainly go on. These are unpleasant, no doubt, but an inevitable part of life. When you are overwhelmed with any of these emotions, it's easy to feel alone. Huddled atop a dark, treacherous, jagged peak of a mountain you never wanted to be on in the first place. Desperately trying to get the hell off that mountain any way you can, doing your best to ignore what got you there in the first place. Recently I was introduced to the idea of welcoming these emotions in. Seeing them. Acknowledging them. Loving them. That may seem like a terrible idea at first. Uncomfortable. Ridiculous. No, thank you. But imagine being up on that treacherous peak once more. This time, however, you're no longer alone but sitting with your friend as the warm glow of the sun peeks through the clouds. The warmth trickles in, filling both of you with the comfort and hope of a new day. Reminding you that experiencing the dark is what allows us all to revel in the light.

True clinical depression forces you somewhere else. There's no peak. No light. No hope for a way out. You are pulled into an endless void surrounding you with voices that speak of nothing but despair. Hopelessness. Helplessness. Unworthiness. In moments that you can muster up any will at all to escape, you quickly realize it's futile. You are chained. Bound. Caged. Laying in defeat. Praying for a way out.

I remember the first time I had thoughts of killing myself. I was eight. I don't remember what led up to it, but I was angry. So angry that I thought I didn't deserve to live. My feet pounded across the floor as I made my way to the kitchen. My hands were tightly clenched into fists. Once there, I forcibly grabbed a knife and held it above my wrist. My body shook as I stood there, trembling. My heavy breath forced my chest up and down, as my eyes stayed steady, fixated on my delicate skin. A few moments went by as I stayed in that exact position, in that exact state, quivering with fury. This thought suddenly flooded my mind: "If I kill myself, God won't love me anymore and I'll go to Hell." I put the knife away and walked out of the kitchen. I no longer believe that we are somehow punished by a vengeful God, but my perfectionism has been a much more difficult ideology to shake. I have come a long way, but I still fight it. I was so incredibly hard on myself, and any perceived imperfection led me straight to feeling completely worthless. Useless. That I should no longer exist. I didn't deserve to.

I desperately tried to hide this part of myself. I never told anyone, including my parents, about my first real thoughts of suicide. When I was eight. Perhaps due to a mixture of shame, and not feeling like I would be listened to or understood. I struggled with not only the feelings that come with depression, but also why I had them in the first place. I couldn't make sense of it. So, I smiled. "I'm fine" became my mantra. If life was a stage, "Put on a Happy Face" was my theme song. If my show was convincing enough, I could fool everyone, including myself. And perhaps, at times, I did. I truly believe at my core, I'm a joyful person who looks for the good in people. Pollyanna was one of my favorite movies growing up and I still have a soft spot for it. This core part of my being got to shine through at times. Others, I had to work harder. Dance faster. Smile bigger. Until I collapsed. When I could no longer keep the performance going, I knew I was in real trouble. I just couldn't do it anymore. And at nineteen years old, I fell. And fell hard.

By this point, I had struggled not only with depression, but also an eating disorder. I started restricting when I was around thirteen. It eventually led to Bulimia. Tenth grade was the first time I got the impulse to cut myself. I'm not exactly sure how, but that message was clear. I sat on top of my toilet in the bathroom with a kitchen knife. I was delicate at first. Scared. Then I tried harder. And harder. The knife wouldn't cut into my skin, so, in my immense frustration, I grabbed a belt. And I beat myself with it. I beat myself until I was red. And bruised. And heartbroken.

I didn't try to cut again. Not until freshman year of college. The impulse had shown up from time to time, but somehow I was able to resist it. Now, it was stronger than I was. I couldn't fight it. And this time, my cuts were successful. Not once. Or twice. But many times. On a few occasions, the impulse gave me a different idea. Something else, I decided, I deserved. I held a lighter in my hand, stared into the flame, and thrust it onto my skin seconds later. As it seared my skin, I was overcome with relief. Then grief. And sadness. So much anger convoluted with despair. By March, Justine, one of my best friends, recognized how much I needed help. She took me to the medical center at UF. It's among one of the many reasons I'm so thankful for her.

That trip to the UF counseling center led to a two week stay in the hospital. I had been cutting myself fairly regularly. Although they were never suicide attempts, the counselor felt I needed more consistent care. She understood that these were cries for help, and felt that I should go to the hospital. The eighth floor of the hospital to be exact. The mental health floor. "Crazy eight" as fellow patients and I would call it with a laugh. But what that laughter tried to hide was immense and insurmountable pain. Pain that lived deep within us and brought us all to the eighth floor. Pain that makes me pause as I write this. It's uncomfortable. And makes me feel incredibly exposed. Knots are twisting and tangling themselves in my belly. They tighten up as I admit to another two week stay a few months later. This time it was in South Florida while I spent the summer at home. And my brain screams "stop writing this" as I recall my two-week visit to an eating disorder clinic during my year hiatus from college. I don't want to reveal all of this. I want to leave it all out. My finger has moved to the delete button numerous times. I worry. Worry what people will think. Worry I won't be believed. After all, my voice has been stifled so many times in my life. Am I just setting myself up for more of that?

My family never seemed to understand. Nor did I

ever feel they really tried to. I love them, and I know they love me, but this was something that I felt often. We never *really* talked about it. And I often felt like they just didn't know what to do with me. I was talked about while in their presence, often with doctors, but no one really asked *me*. My parents were there the first time I was in the hospital, and I remember they were saying, while I was nearby to hear, that they "didn't know what was bothering me" and it "must be the divorce". I remember thinking that wasn't it at all, but it didn't feel like it mattered. Perhaps that isn't true. They came to see me afterall. But I never felt like they tried to actually understand. Understand my pain, or understand me. I can accept that perhaps they didn't know how. But at nineteen, it broke my heart. And as tears well up in my eyes as I write this, I realize it still does.

This realization brings me back to my earlier questions. The worry. Wondering what others will think. If my own parents didn't understand, how can I expect anyone else to? Which makes me want to delete this whole section. But I'm choosing not to. If I'm to tell my story, how can I leave this out? The depression. The self-harm. The hospital visits. It's all part of it. A part that deserves to be told. To tell it fully probably merits its own book, but, for now, I will say that those experiences, particularly in the hospitals, were surreal. Interesting. Heartbreaking. At times, even comical. But no matter what, they belong.

I stop for a moment, gazing at the computer screen. My fingers are momentarily frozen atop the keyboard. I realize I'm taking in all that I've just revealed. Breathing deeper, I notice I'm struggling with what to say next. I realize that I'm filled with sadness. And deep down, I sense a bit of shame that still lingers in the darkness. Shame for treating myself so terribly. But it's important to understand that self-harm creates a cycle. One that starts with anger and sadness. One that is rarely, if ever, about killing oneself. That certainly was the case for me. I certainly had thoughts about suicide, but I never really wanted to die. The act of self harm, however, does create a sense of relief. The release is brief, however, as guilt and shame come rushing in when you think about what you've done to yourself. Anger and sadness settle in once more and the cycle continues. Looking back, I often felt like a pot of boiling water. The pressure would rise as the bubbles moved faster and faster. The lid on the pot would tremble and convulse as the energy swirled beneath it. Pushing and pushing until the intensity was too much to bear. I just didn't know how to release it. But with time, and tools, I've learned better ways to move the energy. And to forgive myself.

My heart hurts for anyone who has experienced this. I understand. And I also know things can change. Depression is still something I must be aware of. Recognize when it starts to creep in. But I know it isn't who I am, nor does it define me. I've had to learn to see it. Welcome it. Acknowledge it. And gently bring it back into the light. Despite the fact I still struggle with it, it doesn't mean I have to accept it as my day-to-day reality. I have choices. I have the choice to get help when I need it. I have the choice to take medication that gives my brain the chemicals it needs to function at its best. I have the choice to know that depression is not bigger than me. Stronger than me. Because, after all, it is not *me*.

In the past, my life performance would have looked something like this:

> The curtain opens to a lone dancer. The spotlight beams down upon her, catching a sparkle from the elaborate beading of her costume. Musical notes begin to flutter through the air. She's calm. Confident. Mesmerizing. Suddenly, a shift comes over her, throwing her off balance. It's slight, but she knows it. And it knocks her out of her joyful expression. Desperation floods her body. She can't let anyone notice. She grabs another layer of costuming. This one has even more sparkles. More flair. Her limbs move faster as she twirls across the stage. She wills her smile to grow bigger, wider, for she knows no one can see you frown. After all, the show *must* go on. Back in the spotlight, her bliss radiates as her body soars. Until another shift happens. And another. And another. Until she is in a frenzy. Her body moves frantically under the numerous layers she has added. Wigs. Masks. Rhinestones. She can no longer bear the weight, or keep up, and she collapses to the ground. Embarrassed. Ashamed. Defeated. A failure.

Now, I imagine the person I am today. Stepping into the end of that performance. Crumpled on the floor. Letting those feelings run over me and drain into the ground. Slowly, steadily, I stand. Removing layers one by one. The wigs. The masks. The rhinestones. Until I am naked. Panic begins to bubble up in my chest as the urge to run and hide in the darkness sweeps over me. But I fight. I fight as I always have, but this time a different ending reveals itself. This time, I don't run. I don't hide. I stay exactly where I am. In the spotlight. Facing the crowd. My body trembles at first, but, as I stand my ground and embrace the light that shines over my body, I become still. Calm. Resolute. Allowing all of me to exist. To be seen. To be known. And all of it is beautiful.

Chapter 5

August 1996

Second Mental Hospital. Male Nurse. Upon finding out I was still a virgin, he told another patient he would happily, "Show me how it's done."

The morning sun trickles into the room, telling me it's time to wake up. I groan and shift my body, resisting the invitation. The hospital sheets feel scratchy beneath my skin. As I inhale, I catch a whiff of that weird smell that's been present ever since I got here. I only have a few days left. And I'm suddenly aware of the excitement and trepidation this thought brings up inside me. Get up. I have to get up. Curled up on my side, I feel the sun's rays brighten a bit against my eyelids. I open my eyes halfway, then let them close again.

Ugggggh, I hate mornings. But someone is going to come by soon and tell me to get up. So I may as well start the process. I slowly, begrudgingly, blink my eyes a few more times. As I do, I see white in front of me. Blink. Blink. Blink. White. A white uniform. Blink. Blink. Blink. Tanned skin. As my vision comes into focus, I can see clearly the man standing in my room. Close to my bed. I look up at him. What the fuck? How long has he been here? This male nurse. The same one another patient warned me about. The nice guy that seemed to want to look out for me. He left yesterday. But he told me. He told me not to trust this male nurse. Because of the things he said about me. The things he said he'd like to do to me. Oh my God.

Silently, slowly, he leans his body in a little closer. His eyes narrow. He coos, softy, "You're sooooooooo pretty when you're sleeping." He smiles, a sly, closed mouth smile, eyes burning through me as I look up at him. Frozen. Dumbfounded. He turns, with the same slimy expression, and quietly strolls out of my room. I don't move. I feel my heart beat louder. Ringing through my ears. My stomach turns. I feel disgusting. Gone is any fear of leaving this hospital. This place that was supposed to help me. Filled with people who were supposed to help me. If anything happens, who will believe me? No one. I'm alone. Alone in a mental hospital. Voiceless. Powerless. Exposed.

I need to get the fuck out of here.

Chapter 6

Spring 1998

Mother's Day was approaching. We had one week off before the summer semester started. My car had been overheating a bit, but after two trips to the mechanic, they couldn't find anything wrong. My father suggested I take it to the shop in Boca since they had worked on the car previously. It sounded good enough to me, so I decided to make the trip home.

As I started the four hour ride from Gainesville to Boca, I couldn't help but reflect on my first semester as a dance major. Despite a bad strain to one of my adductor muscles, my heart was full. I had terrific friends. Friends that not only worked hard, but also had a lot of fun. I had professors that were incredibly supportive. Professors that challenged me, but also nurtured me. And accepted me. I truly felt seen. Not only for my dance abilities, but also for my choreography. My close friend and I had choreographed a duet together. One that seemed to touch many. We named it Porcelain; it was about our struggle with Bulimia. It won a few awards and was selected to represent the University at the American College Dance Festival. I was honored. Thrilled. I may have done a few cartwheels.

During the festival, I witnessed many beautiful works of art and took classes that were both challenging and fun. After a few days, my friends and I gathered to listen to the adjudicators give feedback about the various dances that were performed. They were also announcing which pieces would move forward to the "highlights" concert. Tears of joy streamed down my face when I heard them announce "Porcelain." Sincere celebration took place for all of us that day as we hugged and wooed gleefully. I swear at that moment, I could hear the chains that had bound me in depression for so long, break off and fall away.

Two hours into my drive, I pulled off just past Orlando at a rest stop. My car was running a little hot, but seemed okay. After I filled it with gas and started to drive away, the needle suddenly went all the way into the red as the engine yelled, "Clink, clunk, I'm too damn hot!" My heart sank as I pulled over. I got out of my car and started walking the mile back to the station in the warm Florida sun. Shortly, an older couple pulled over and asked if I needed a ride. I told them where I was headed and they wanted to help me get there. Normally, I wouldn't dream of getting into a car with strangers, but at that moment I felt safe. They were warm and kind, so I climbed in. After they dropped me off, I smiled and waved as they left, thankful for their graciousness. I called a tow truck. Then I called my brother who lived in Orlando. He wasn't home. I didn't have a cell phone, yet, so it wasn't as easy as it is now. I waited. And waited. And waited. Three hours later, I had no luck reaching my brother and no tow truck was in sight. I had reached my limit and decided to try and continue home. At a food vendor, I asked the girl behind the counter for two large cups. I told her my situation and that I was going to fill the cups with water for my car. I was grateful she took pity on me and agreed to my request. As I started the walk back to my car, a single middle aged male in a silver Corvette pulled over and asked if I needed a ride. Again, I wondered if this was a good idea. I looked down at his hands and he was holding a cup of frozen yogurt. It was starting to melt. I'm not sure why, but seeing that made me comfortable enough to accept. He dropped me off at my little blue car, all alone on the side of the road. I thanked him and watched him pull away. I poured the water into the car, and pulled out onto the road.

An hour later, I pulled into a gas station and told the clerk that my car was running hot and asked if he could help me. He had a small bottle of coolant and another of oil. They had both been opened, but were mostly full. He told me I could have them.

"Really?" I asked in disbelief. He nodded yes. "Are

you sure?" Again, he assured me I could have them. I was taken aback, but so thankful. I had been shown so much kindness on this day. I thought about each person who had helped me. I was touched. Warmed. Delighted. My belief that humans are mostly good was solidified. Proof that deep down, people are kind hearted and generous of spirit.

I finally made it home. I was glad to be there. I had worked at a drug store the summer before my freshman year, and they would let me pick up a few shifts here and there when I was home. I worked there on Wednesday. Thursday, I went to the mall to get my mom her present. I also found a cute bikini; something that was rare for me to buy or feel comfortable in. But I was actually excited about it. Friday morning, I worked again. Early. 5:30am. My dad was flying into town and said he would pick me up. His flight got delayed, and he didn't get there until 5:30pm. Finally, he walked in and I was relieved to get done with my twelve hour shift. We went to an Italian restaurant and had a delicious, albeit heavy meal. Man, I miss gluten!

When I got home, I sat on the floor next to my bed and talked to a friend on the phone. A Garfield phone I had gotten for my tenth birthday. I absolutely loved that phone. I still remember how excited I was when I got it. I told her about my long day, as well as my road trip shenanigans. She fussed at me for getting into a car with strangers.

"Don't you know that's how people get killed?" she asked me.

"I know, I know," I replied. "But everyone was so nice. It kind of reinvigorated my faith in humanity."

Exhausted, I climbed into bed. My mom was still out with her friends. I, the college student, was home. Listening to my brand new Tori Amos CD on repeat. Her haunting, beautiful voice filled my bedroom. Her heartfelt lyrics swirling all around me, her passionate vocals pulsating through the air.

As I lay on my stomach, I noticed the fullness that lingered in my belly from dinner. And while Tori sang me off to sleep, I never imagined that meal could have been my last.

Chapter 7

May 9, 1998

Approximately 2:30am

My eyes start to blink open. My head feels heavy. My chin reaches for my chest as it gently rocks and sways. My mind searches, still half asleep, as to why my head is no longer on my pillow. I feel strong hands wrapped around my breasts, lifting my body, half slumped over, heavy with sleep.

"Don't worry," a deep voice says, "I'm a friend of your mother's."

This deep voice travels from close behind me. Thoughts race through my mind, faster than a bolt of lightning. *Is she okay? Did she bring someone home with her? No, no, there's no way.* I am now sitting on the bed, feet reaching the floor, feeling his body next to mine. My eyes grow wide as I turn my torso to the left. I take in his silhouette, lit by the one narrow moon beam that streams through my broken vertical blind. I inhale deeply, bring my clenched hands up to the sides of my head, bend my torso as my knees come towards my chest, and scream.

My scream begins to permeate the air as my arms and legs move back and forth, like I'm running. Running harder than I ever have in my life. My body stays folded over. And I scream. I feel this hard jab at my side. Towards my lower back. Like he's punched me. And I scream. My screams form the words, "Mom, 911, Mom, 911" and I scream. Over and over and over. I keep screaming. I keep flailing. I keep fighting.

Still screaming for my mother, I sense he is no longer next to me. I look up and see him running towards my bedroom door. I stand up. My eyes follow him as he runs beyond the doorway, to the left, and out of sight. My gaze descends and finds the light beige carpet. It travels this beige sea and finds my feet, continues up my ankles, up my legs, and stops at my lower torso. Blood. So much blood. Rushing down. Gushing out of my body.

I stare as blood pours down my legs, and suddenly light floods the hallway next to my room. I look up and see my mother.

"A man stabbed me; a man stabbed me. Call 911."

"There's no man here," she replies in her southern accent.

"Just go call 911!" I yell.

She runs out of my room, to hers. I look down again. I'm dying. Oh my God, I'm dying.

She flies past my room as I hear, "The phone's off the hook."

If I don't get an ambulance here, now, I'm dead. I look to my right and see the Garfield phone on the floor, next to my bed, where I had left it the night before. I fall to it. Lift the receiver. And listen to my mother talking to a dispatcher. Oh, thank God. I place the receiver down on the floor.

My mother rushes in. I start asking aloud, confused and desperate, "Why did he stab me? Why did he stab me?"

She grabs my leg. Startled, I look up. "What are you doing?" I ask.

She has a towel in her hand. "I'm trying to make a tourniquet," she replies.

I sigh. "OK." I lay my head back down on the floor. Where are they? Why isn't the ambulance here yet? If they don't get here, I am going to die. "I'm dying. Oh my God, I'm dying. Where are they?" I plea. It feels like time is painfully slow and moving at warp speed, all around me. "Why is this happening to me? Why did he stab me? Why aren't they here, yet?"

Suddenly, a beam of light hits my face. Squinting, I look towards the source coming from my doorway. A man holding a flashlight says, "We're here to take care of you, okay?"

I nod, and utter weakly, "Okay." I'm exhausted. Confused. Scared. Desperate to get to the hospital. Suddenly, a group of men surrounds me. One puts an oxygen mask over my mouth. Another starts to grab my leg. I try to move my foot and realize I can't.

Panicked, I yell out, "I can't move my foot. Am I paralyzed?"

He slides something up and down my lower leg and asks, "Can you feel this?"

"Yes," I reply, and he tells me I'm going to be okay.

A brief sigh of relief washes over me, but it is short lived in the encompassing turmoil. I manage to hear, "We've got more" amongst the voices so intently focused on helping me. I realize my shirt is being cut off, and any impulse of modesty I would normally feel is quickly tossed aside. With gravity in his voice, he calls out, "We've got another one." I hear a simple reply.

"Oh my God." I take note of the disbelief in his voice, sprinkled with uncertainty and bewilderment. I suddenly feel my stomach, spinning, churning, mirroring the chaos whirling around me. "I'm going to throw up. I'm going to throw up."

I pull the mask off, vomit, and immediately regret the big Italian dinner I had enjoyed earlier. One of them says, "Y'all know I can't handle throw- up."

"I'm sorry," I said.

Voices assure me it's okay.

"I'm sorry. It's gross."

I'm unsure as to how much time has passed at this point. "We're going to move you onto this board, okay? One, two, three."

My body is swiftly picked up and placed back down. My body floats up once again, and this time, stops midway from the floor; I'm levitating. Grateful to be heading to the hospital, I close my eyes. I trust these men will get me there. I feel my body, supported by this board I'm being carried on, move out of my bedroom and down the short hallway. I sense I'm near the front door as we turn the corner. Abruptly, the board shakes beneath me and I hear glass smash onto the floor. The sound pulls my focus to the right, looking towards the empty space on the wall where a picture was just moments ago. I notice a woman at the end of the hall, standing next to my room wearing a white gown. I stare for just a moment. It's my mother. I should say something to her, but I can't. Hospital. I need to get to the hospital. I sigh heavily as I turn my face back towards the ceiling and refocus. Hospital. I need to get to the hospital. Now. It's the only way I'm going to survive.

In the ambulance, exhaustion overtakes me. I mutter, "Why did he stab me?" to anyone who will listen. I desperately want someone to explain this ordeal to me. I just can't comprehend it. My eyelids fall. Heavy. It feels so hard to breathe. Like there's an elephant sitting on my chest. I'm so tired.

"Can you open your eyes, sweetheart?" I try. They blink a few times, and close again.

"I'm sorry," I say. "I can't. But I'm here."

They tell me, "Okay, but we need you to stay awake, okay? Stay with us." I nod. A few seconds go by. "Are you still with us?"

I nod yes. I ask again for someone to tell me why. Why is this happening to me? No one has the answer. Without warning, I feel a draining sensation rush from my head as my eyes flutter. My left cheek swiftly falls towards my shoulder as unconsciousness threatens to overtake me. A shout rings through the air, "No, no, no, don't fall asleep!"

I whip my head back. I whisper, "I'm here. I'm here."

Chapter 8

Early June 1998

Sitting in the living room with my mother, I look over at the wall. All of the pictures are in their place. All but one. The empty space is a blatant reminder. And it seems a bit desperate to be put back whole again.

"I guess you haven't replaced the picture frame the paramedics broke carrying me out?"

"No, I haven't," she replies simply.

"You were in the hallway when they carried me out, right?"

"No," she says as she shakes her head. Confusion creeps across my face.

"You weren't? I looked over after they knocked the picture off the wall and thought you were standing at the end of the hallway."

"No," she answers again.

"Really? Weren't you wearing your long white nightgown?"

She shakes her head again. "No, the police kept me in my bedroom. They didn't let me come out to watch you go."

Huh. My mother got up and walked out of the room. I sat there, recalling seeing her. At least I thought it was her. I know I saw a woman with a white gown. Wait, there was blue. Yes, a blue and white gown. Were they blue sashes? I think they were. And she had dark, shoulder length hair. Not the red hair my mom has. Huh. And...... no face. She didn't have a face. Weird. So there was a woman with no face, shoulder length dark hair, and a white silk looking gown with thick blue sashes running down the front of her gown. Huh. I think.....was that? I think I saw an angel.....

Chapter 9

May 9, 1998

Early Morning

Emergency Room

I don't remember getting here. The lights above me are bright, and my eyes blink rapidly a few times in response. The metal beneath me is cold. Unfamiliar. Unforgiving. Voices are buzzing around me, and although they are steady and controlled, I can sense the urgency that encapsulates their tones. I feel a tugging at my ears. As I look over, a nurse asks, "Do you have any other piercings?"

"No," I reply.

"All of your jewelry will be in a bag for you," she reassures me.

I give a slight smile and a nod. I hear another voice call out, "She needs blood, she needs blood."

My survival mode swiftly returns, strengthening my

voice. "Negative AB," I exclaim.

The same nurse looks at me and repeats, "Negative AB?"

"Yes," I reply, and emphatically repeat, "Negative AB." Her voice rings out to the rest, "She's negative AB, negative AB."

As bodies and voices swirl around me, a man introduces himself as the doctor, informs me of my location, and that they are going to do everything they can to help. I estimate he's kind, determined, and authoritative, and I simply reply, "Hi. Thank you." For a few seconds, I'm calm. Like I'm in a little boat that shelters me from the raging seas that thrash and claw, desperate to overtake me. But I feel safe. Serene. Trusting in the protection of the strong wood that surrounds me. But the sea is powerful and resolute. Suddenly, a huge wave takes me. It grabs my legs, thrusting my pelvis into the air. I look down, quizzically, to see a nurse, holding one leg over her shoulder, spreading my legs open. Her fingers are poking around inside my vagina. She looks up, and sees my face contorted and confused.

"Oh, I'm just inserting your catheter," she says with a smile that is apologetically sympathetic.

"Okay," I reply as I lay my head back down, aware of the awkwardness I feel.

I hear them call for a plastic surgeon and an orthopedic surgeon. I'm asked to drink some sort of liquid. They insert the straw past my lips, and I sip.

"Ugh," I say as I retract from the straw.

"I know it's gross, but we need you to drink this so we can see if you have any internal bleeding." I nod and will myself to drink it down. So much is going on around me it's hard to keep track. I'm exhausted. The orthopedic surgeon arrives and asks me to lift each finger on my left hand. I try. One by one. And each time, I fail. My pinky finger is the only one that barely cooperates as it shakes and lifts a tiny amount. He asks me again to try. Each finger. The same result. Such a simple task, yet I'm unable to find the strength or ability to perform it. I tell him I'm done. I've tried. I can't do it.

Again, the sea rushes around me, making it difficult to focus. So much energy, turmoil, and chaos. I manage to feel a bit of tugging near my left ear, as the plastic surgeon alerts me to his presence. He is quick to announce, "Well, I'm done."

It seems like an impossibly short amount of time, but my attention is rapidly drawn to my abdomen. The doctor is rubbing something around my belly and informs me they are going to check for bleeding. "I'm going to insert this tube through your belly button and you're probably going to feel some pressure." Instantly, I do. I feel the hard tube. Jabbing. Pounding. Slamming against the inside of my stomach. I quickly realize I don't want to feel any of this anymore. I cry out, and he apologizes for his aggressiveness. "I'm sorry, but we have to make sure."

Desperate, I ask, "Can I be put to sleep?"

"I'm sorry, we can't do that just yet," he replies.

I nod. "Okay." The hammering inside of my stomach

continues and I'm compelled to ask again. "Can I be put to sleep, now?"

He repeats himself and adds, "If we put you to sleep, there's a greater chance you won't wake up. So, we need to wait, okay?"

I sigh, and once again nod. "Okay, thank you."

I'm tired. So tired of thrashing around in this turbulent ocean of uncertainty and pain. But also thankful for the people surrounding me in it. I realize the doctor is now standing closer to my face, and I can see the concern and exhaustion in his expression. "We are going to take you to get a scan to check out your internal organs. This way, we can get a better idea of what you might need surgically without completely opening you up."

I nod and feel the bed begin to move. Before long, it glides smoothly down the halls, with the tireless crew of my ship guiding the way. We reach the destination quickly, and I can see the large machine when I roll my eyes up and back.

"We're going to send you into the machine, now."

But I can't go in. The waves of the sea have taken over my body. I feel sick. "I'm going to throw up. Wait. I'm going to throw up." I turn my head to the side, and vomit erupts from my core. As the vomit spills on the floor, I notice something else. Another substance. Red. Blood. Oh my God. Blood is once again spilling out of me. I whip my head back up and yell out, "I'm bleeding! I'm bleeding!"

The nurse closest to me realizes what I'm saying. Looking at me, she asks, "You're bleeding?" and instantly turns to the others and yells out, "She's bleeding, she's bleeding."

I hear the doctor shout, "We have to get her into surgery, now!"

They swiftly move into action, racing against time. I hear their feet, pounding the hard floor as they run into battle. The lights on the ceiling dash by, one by one, hitting my eyes like a camera flash. "Stay with us, Lynn, stay with us."

With each flash, I feel more and more life drain out of me. I'm cold. So very cold. It's unlike anything I've ever felt. I look up at the nurse, fear and desperation stretched across my face, pleading for help. Looking down at me, she says, "Your lips are blue."

"I'm really cold," I softly tell her.

She turns to everyone. "Her lips are blue," she says and they run faster. "Hang on, okay? Hang on." Time, once again, is painfully slow and overwhelmingly fast in this strange vortex I've found myself in.

The bed comes to a stop, and the whirlwind continues around me. The doctor tells me, "You get to go to sleep now, okay?" I weakly nod and whisper, "Thank you" as he brings an oxygen mask up to my face. I'm thankful. Thankful for these people who are with me, working so hard to save my life. I return to the little boat that kept me calm before with its strong, sturdy wood. It gently cradles me as my eyes flutter and close. And we begin to descend. As I swiftly sink further into oblivion, I'm thankful I can finally go to sleep.

Chapter 10

Sustained Injuries from multiple stab wounds

1. Laceration to the left preauricular (between the ear lobe and the face) area.
2. Laceration posterior neck overlaying the cervical vertebral bodies.
3. Stab wound to the left chest at the posterior axillary line approximately the 9th intercostal space. (Between the ribs.)
4. Stab wound to left posterior flank. Left diaphragmatic tear and injury to splenic hilum.
5. Stab wound to the left thoraco-abdomen with hemodynamic instability.
6. Laceration of the dorsal of left wrist. Full laceration of all extensor tendons, as well as underlying muscle. It was noted that chips of bone were missing.

7. Stab wound to the lateral aspect of the left leg at approximately the level of the knee. The peroneal nerve was severed. Some of the underlying gastroc muscle was found to be lacerated and herniated.

Chapter 11

Surgical Procedure

1. Developed hypovolemic shock/became hemodynamically unstable and was aggressively resuscitated before taken to the operating room.
2. Exploratory laparotomy
3. Splenectomy
4. Ligation of the transected splenic artery.
5. Repair of left hemidiaphragm.
6. Left tube thoracostomy.
7. Multiple left extensor tendon repair
8. Left peroneal nerve repair

Estimated total blood loss: 21 pints

Chapter 12

Sixteen days in the Hospital, May 1998

I'm not exactly sure where to begin. It was long. And strange. And, although this may sound weird, filled with both kindness and animosity from the hospital staff. I felt extremely vulnerable. Exposed. Helpless. I was completely dependent on others for at least the first half of my stay, which felt awful to me. I was strong. Independent. And even though I had suffered greatly, I was, and still am, a fighter. I don't give up. And this experience would prove to be no different.

I was in the Intensive Care Unit for nine days. I was placed in the pediatric room, which meant it was private. Not my choice, obviously, but I was told later on they didn't have room elsewhere and there were no children in ICU at the time. I was on life support, feeding tubes, and morphine, for the first five days after the initial emergency surgery. I slept a lot, especially the first 48 hours or so. I recall being awake here and there, and can remember some of the visits I had while intubated. One of the emergency nurses came to check on me the day after my surgery. It was a brief moment, but I managed to wake up for it. She told me who she was, and that she liked to come check on her patients. I was so out of it, and tried to respond the best I could, but I quickly passed back out. That moment of kindness still stays with me, though.

No one was certain for the first few days if I would live or not. But like I said, I'm a fighter. By the afternoon of the fifth day, May 13th, it was clear that I could breathe enough on my own. My feeding tube was removed and I was taken off life support. Because of this, they also took me off of morphine. I was given a Demerol drip instead, but I swear it barely worked. I was in constant pain. I kept telling the nurses, but they just seemed annoyed with me. I found out later (from the notes written by the hospital's psychiatrist) that they felt I was "dramatic" at times, I was trying to abuse my pain meds, and I exhibited signs of drug seeking. I was livid when I read this. I still am. In 1992, the Agency for Healthcare Policy and Research, recommended morphine as the drug of choice rather than Demerol in preventing and controlling acute postoperative pain. One of the major reasons was that an estimated fifty percent of surgical patients experienced moderate to severe pain post operatively. [1]If this federal guideline was published in 1992, why was this hospital still using

Demerol for post operative care? I obviously wasn't drug seeking. I was in excruciating pain. But once again, my voice was stifled.

Like most dancers, I think I have a high pain tolerance. For better or worse, we work our bodies tirelessly, and tend to "dance through" a lot of injuries and discomfort. But I had never experienced anything like this. My whole body felt like it was on fire. Everything hurt. My skin was stretched thin from every inch of me being swollen. And by swollen, I mean unrecognizable (as I was later told). I had so many tubes coming out of my body. The ones running down my throat and my nose had been removed. But my heart, my urethra, my pancreas, and my lungs still had them. I had been cut open from the tip of my sternum to a few inches above my pubic bone. Staples kept my skin together. Not just from my surgical scar, but also where my stab wounds were. All seven of them. Well, six I suppose, since one of them had a chest tube thrust through it. Those are horrible. Every breath I took produced a sharp pain as my lungs and ribs started to expand. The scar tissue in my lungs still reminds me of it from time to time when I get that same sensation. I also remember feeling like my mouth was a desert. It was so dry, I could barely swallow. And I was constantly lying in my own sweat. It felt so hot to me. Sweltering. Miserable. My mom told me later that I smelled bad. She could smell me as soon as she got into the doorway.

On May 14, I was still low on blood and I needed to

go into surgery to repair all of the extensor tendons on my left wrist, and the peroneal nerve in my left leg. I received two more pints of blood, and my God, I was in so much pain afterwards. I'm not sure why, but it was horrible. The nice man that came to get me to take me to surgery could see it all over my face. I was only with him for a few moments, but his kindness and soothing energy made an impression that has stayed with me. My surgeon was also incredible. He was young, passionate, and clearly a very skilled and talented surgeon. I'm thankful everyday for him.

Back in my hospital bed, multiple surgeries later, I thought the absolute worst was over. I knew I had a long road ahead of me, but surely it would get better. Little did I know, I would be hit with something extremely unexpected. When I think back to the day-time nurses in particular, they generally seemed annoyed they had to deal with me. I felt like they had some animosity towards me, and I never understood why. It didn't go unnoticed by my friends and family, either. I was only allowed visitation for 30 minutes, 3 times per day. But they could see how I was being treated. They told me that most of the other people in the ICU were in commas, or couldn't talk for one reason or another. (Apparently, they had to walk by all of the other patients to come see me.). Maybe that's why they were annoyed and gruff? Or was it something else? I was unaware, perhaps naively, that my history would be broadcast to the entire staff. Suddenly, I felt like everyone knew every "bad, shameful" thing about me.

Which made me wonder. Maybe they weren't annoyed because I could communicate with them. Maybe it was because they were told I was someone with a history of Major Depression and Bulimia. And that it was severe enough in the past that I had been hospitalized for it. But why should that affect how they treated me? I was brutally attacked. I had been stabbed seven times. I lost 21 pints of blood. I fought to be here. I lived. The fact that I didn't want to die seemed rather obvious to me. How could anyone think otherwise?

I was made aware of this possibility when I had to speak to the hospital's psychiatrist, a day after I was taken off life support. I don't remember him coming across as a warm, caring man. But I answered his questions the best I could, even though I didn't totally see why my history had anything to do with my current situation. I'll be honest that I can't remember most of the conversation, but the following I recall quite clearly. Towards the end of his questioning, he looked up and asked, "Did you do this to yourself?"

I was stunned. Flabbergasted. Hurt. I truly couldn't believe it. How could my injuries be self-inflicted? I replied, emphatically, "No!"

He quickly replied, "Well, you've done things like this before."

I strongly, forcefully, replied, "Like this??? I don't think so."

And he left. I watched this man just stand up and leave after he accused me of stabbing myself. And all I could do was lie there. Bewildered. Heart-broken. And angry. So incredibly angry. And for the first time, I realized that some of the people in that hospital, people who were supposed to care for me and help me, didn't believe me. And later, I would have to continue to prove my innocence to the police. To this day I question which is worse. Getting brutally attacked or not being believed it happened at all.

Stunned and saddened by my visit from the psychiatrist, I told my dad I didn't want to see him ever again. My dad told me he talked to him some time later. He said, "You really upset my daughter....She is also right-handed and has a stab wound in the left side of her back. Do you think she is triple jointed or something?"

The psychiatrist apparently responded, "I didn't know she had a stab wound in her back."

My father also told me he talked to my attending surgeon about the psychiatrist. The surgeon told him, "She wouldn't be here if she didn't want to be. She fought to be here. That's why she's alive."

As happy as that made me feel to know the surgeon said that, I also knew that was the truth. So why didn't everyone else? I knew I still had a long way to go to get better, and I needed to focus on that. The day nurses, at least from my perspective, had been, and continued to be, unsympathetic overall. I remember the first day they made me get out of bed and sit in a chair. I was told it was necessary and that since I no longer had a feeding tube, I needed to eat. I don't doubt any of that is true. But I needed help. A lot of it. The nurse that was assisting me at the time was impatient and forceful. I worked hard to get out of bed. It was exhausting. And rather painful. With a lot of difficulty, I sat up in bed and hobbled to the chair. I did it. And the nurse proceeded to put a chicken dinner in front of me to eat. The room was spinning. I started drooling. And shaking. Uncontrollably. She didn't seem to care when she told me I needed to eat. I tried. I told her I was trying. But I just couldn't. Still shaking and drooling, she grabbed my plate. Disappointed I didn't eat. I think I even apologized. It was terrible.

Later that evening, the night nurse was much kinder. She told me she heard how the day went. She also knew of my history with Bulimia. I told her that wasn't the issue here. I told her what my experience was like. I also explained that I was unsure how I was expected to eat all of that given the state I was in. Especially after I had a feeding tube for almost a week. She seemed to understand. She brought me crackers and applesauce. And shaved my legs. I recall being thankful whenever she was there. She was patient and sympathetic. I'm still grateful for her.

I'm also beyond thankful to those that were there the night I was brought in. I can't imagine how tirelessly they worked. One day, towards the end of my ICU stay, I had slept through the once daily visit by a doctor. It happened to be the same doctor that performed my emergency surgery. Shortly after, an assisting physician was checking on me, and informed me I had slept through the visit. I asked if he could tell the doctor to come back. The assistant explained that the doctor's really busy, and it's hard for them to do that. I told him it was important. The assistant agreed and my emergency surgeon came back. He sat on the bed, and asked how he could help me. I told him I simply wanted to thank him. I was so grateful for all he and his team had done for me. I obviously didn't know everyone's name, but I hoped he could pass on the message for me. He said he would, gave me a smile, and left. It was a brief conversation, but one that I couldn't go without.

Nine days after being admitted to the ICU, I was told I was being moved to the step down ICU. The nurse declared, "You need to free up the room. You know, for someone who really needs it."

I was thankful to be in another section of the hospital. With different nurses. All of them would look at me with surprise and exclaim, "You're so young! Most of our patients are here after heart surgery." I found it odd that I had to tell all of them why I was there. Wasn't that in my chart? I was met with a few different reactions. One asked me if I was in a gang. Others seemed horrified. One quickly stopped in her tracks with a sharp inhale. She proceeded to tell me that, three weeks prior, someone in her apartment building had been bludgeoned half to death with a pipe iron in the elevator. Once she recovered, she got the hell out of town and moved to California. We both wondered if it was the same attacker.

Each day, I got stronger. I had the most wonderful

Physical Therapist. She was supportive, gentle, and encouraging. She pushed me, but listened when I said, "That's enough." The first day I practiced walking, I could only get to the door. The next day, I made it into the hall. Then, rather quickly, I was walking (with assistance) around the floor of the hospital. She was thrilled. She made me feel accomplished, no matter how little or much I did. Thinking about her makes my chest warm. So much of a person's recovery is mindset, and she was among those who rooted for me.

While in the step down ICU, I had moments of severe dehydration, anemia, and sudden vomiting. I vomited every other day without warning. One of those days happened to be when I got my chest tube out. I had thrown up on myself, but the attending nurse told me there was no time to clean it up because if I missed the doctor, I would have to wait until tomorrow. I had already had that thing for twelve days. I wanted it out. I then asked the nurse if it would hurt. He paused, then asked, "Do you remember getting it put in?"

I told him I didn't, to which he responded, "Oh, well, that's waaaay worse, so you should be fine." I just kind of laughed as my anxiety grew. The doctor came in and explained everything to me. He also told me it might hurt, but he was sure I'd be glad to get it removed. He grabbed hold of the tube while the nurse held my hand. He told me to take a huge breath in as they both did it with me. He said, "Okay, now release it." We all did. Nothing happened. He repeated, "Okay, take the biggest breath you've ever taken in your entire life and hold it." All three of us took a huge inhale as I squeezed the nurse's hand. He forcefully yanked that tube out of my chest.

I yelled, "Jesus Christ. Holy shit!!"

I'm pretty sure it reverberated down the hall. They started laughing. Which made me chuckle. It was quick, but *far* from painless. Despite that, however, I still get a laugh when I think about it today.

After sixteen days in the hospital, I was ready to leave. I asked the physician tending to me that day if I could go home. He spoke to a few different people, and they agreed I could be discharged. I didn't think about how difficult it would be to go back to my mother's house, but I was ready to try. And ready to take a proper shower.

During my long hospital stay, I'm grateful for all of the visits, calls, and cards I received. One of my close friends (the same one who took me to seek care at UF) was away studying in Israel. Her mom came to see me almost every day to report back to her. Many of my friends drove down from Gainesville to visit. Others who were close by came multiple times. I was, and always will be, overwhelmed by the kindness and love I received. To the friends, family, and staff that genuinely cared for and supported me: it still means the world to me and I'll be forever grateful.

---

1. The Pink Sheet. March 9, 1992. Morphine is drug of choice over Demerol for post-op acute pain, first AHCPR guideline recommends: report calls for more aggressive, proactive pain manage-

ment https://pink.pharmaintelligence.informa.com/PS020528/MORPHINE-IS-DRUG-OF-CHOICE-OVER-DEMEROL-FOR-POSTOP-ACUTE-PAIN-FIRST-AHCPR-GUIDELINE-RECOMMENDS-REPORT-CALLS-FOR-AGGRESSIVE-PROACTIVE-PAIN-MANAGEMENT

Chapter 13

Late May 1998

Third Day Home. First Morning Alone.

"Hang on, Mom, someone's on the other line." I click over and answer, "Hello?"

"Hi, is Patricia there?" a male's voice responds.

A twinge of confusion creeps in, but I answer with the rehearsed response I was taught as a child. "She's not able to come to the phone right now." And then I stop. I'm not sure why. Normally I would follow up with "Who may I ask is calling?" But for some reason I don't. The words don't make it out of my mouth. Tension creeps in, tracing up my spine.

"Is this Lynn?" he continues.

My brow furrows with bewilderment. Distrust. I answer, almost feeling like the words are coming out without my choice.

"Yes, it is." A quick pause. Then I hear, "What are the

police doing for you?" His tone is calm. Eerie. I feel like I'm being sucked into a tunnel. My heart beats louder. I can feel it. Can he hear it? My reply is quick. Vague. Careful not to reveal much. "I don't know. I haven't talked to them in a while."

My fingers clasp the phone in desperation as I press the receiver to my ear. I hear him take a quick, short inhale before he speaks.

"Why did you start screaming?" His tone is cocky. Intense. Direct. Unbelievable.

Anger rises swiftly up my body. So does panic.

"Who the fuck is this?" I force through the phone. I knew. My God, I knew it was him all along. Why didn't I react sooner? Where is he right now? Do I hide? Get my mother's gun? Fuck, fuck, fuck.

"Why did you start screaming?" His voice is more forceful this time while making sure to pronounce each word with exact precision. His refined composure is melting away. What lies beneath is revealing itself.

Shaking from both anger and fear, I yell, "WHO THE FUCK IS THIS?"

His patience has vanished. He's angry I lived. That much is clear as he yells with insidious hate, "WHY DID YOU START SCREAMING?"

Tears pour down my face as I click back over to my mother. Then to 911. The detective shows up and he places a monitoring device on my phone. He doesn't believe it was him. He suggests it could have been anyone. Someone pulling a prank perhaps. But this detective didn't hear the venom that poured from his lips as he yelled, "Why did you start screaming?" at me. Over and over again.

That was the only time he called. But I'll never forget it.

Chapter 14

Police. The Predator

I woke up in the hospital, shortly after being taken off life support, to find a man sitting in my room. He introduced himself as the lead detective on my case and began questioning me about the night I was attacked. I told him exactly what I remembered. The fondling. My fear of being raped. I started screaming and flailing. He started stabbing me. I kept screaming. And screaming. Until he eventually fled.

He listened as he took notes. He then started to ask me questions about my mother. Was it possible she did this? That it was her and not a man after all. It was late. I was asleep. I adamantly responded that a man did this, not my mother. He proceeded to tell me that he listened to the recordings from the 911 call, and that both me and my mother could be clearly heard. At one point, it seemed like she was hurting me because I asked, "What are you doing?" It was the most logical explanation, he reasoned. Why else would I have asked that? I told him I remembered and could explain. I was lying on the floor, and I felt her grab my leg. I looked up at her and asked what she was doing. She told me she was trying to wrap a towel around my leg. That it was bleeding. I simply replied, "Oh, okay," and laid back down.

He continued to explain that crimes like this happen in families. And when it occurs amongst close family members, like a mother and daughter, one often lies to protect the other. This would explain why I was heard saying, "Why did *you* stab me? Why did *you* stab me?" I firmly responded, "No. I was saying why did *he* stab me, why did *he* stab me? Because a man did this. And I couldn't understand why."

He wasn't convinced. He asked again if I was protecting her. After all, she was my mother and it was understandable. He also proceeded to tell me that she didn't seem that concerned about me at the police station. She only asked about me once the entire night. And that seemed strange to him. So, if she was the one who stabbed me, I should tell him. I had had enough. I looked him square in the eye and stated, "If my mother did this, I would have absolutely no problem telling you to put that bitch in jail. She didn't do it. A man did this. So stop asking me if my mother stabbed me and find the man that did."

I understand that the police have to do their job. Explore all possibilities. And, unfortunately, violent crimes happen amongst family members. But it doesn't make it any less frustrating and disheartening to go through it. The endless questioning. Constantly trying to prove my own innocence. The feeling of being manipulated and pinned against others. I was asked, over and over, if she attacked me. She was asked if I attacked myself. She told me they kept her at the police station all night. She was exhausted. She disagreed with the detective's statements that she wasn't concerned about me. She did ask about me. However, she wasn't able to deny admitting she thought it might be possible I had stabbed myself. Even though this was completely different than anything that had ever happened before. When I pressed her, obviously hurt and angry, she defensively replied, "Well, what did you expect?"

And with that, it seemed, the conversation was over. I know she went through a lot as well, and I won't profess otherwise. But that hurt me deeply. I read later in the hospital's psychiatrist report that she didn't believe I did this to myself. She said it was very uncharacteristic of my past behavior and that I had been doing much better over the last six months to a year. I can understand logically that she was exhausted and overall unaware of all of the injuries I had sustained. I'm sure they grilled her for hours about it. But it's still painful. And I suppose in regards to her question, I expected her to defend my innocence as I had defended hers.

Once I got out of the hospital, I made multiple trips to the police station to be questioned. Photographed. I felt like I answered the same questions over and over. One topic was common. Had I drank any alcohol? Had I done any drugs? A large bottle of (unopened) wine was in the fridge. Was that mine? Had I had any wine that night? I kept telling him that I was only visiting. It was my mother's house. My mother's wine. I don't even like most wines, including that one. I couldn't understand why I kept having to answer the same question over and over. If this was going to be such an issue, why didn't they just grab a sample of my blood and test it? There was plenty available. Then they would know. And I wouldn't have to defend myself over and over again about it.

The lowest point came when I was asked to take a lie detector test. A FUCKING lie detector test. Of course, I said yes. How would it look to say otherwise? I was so angry. I had been told by the detective that people have done this to themselves. I told him I found that hard to believe. That someone would have to be completely out of their mind. And I wasn't. The officer administering the test said the same thing. I responded similarly. I was shaking. I wanted to pick up that stupid machine and throw it across the room. Watch it smash against the wall. Explode into a million pieces. It was insulting. Degrading. Heartbreaking. And again causes me to question: which is worse? Being brutally stabbed by a stranger or having no one believe you?

Incidentally, my mom had a friend who was transitioning from being a police officer into becoming a therapist. He was still an active policeman for the Palm Beach

County division. He couldn't actively help with my case, however, because my mom's house was within the city limits of Boca Raton. Therefore, we were working with that police force. He would try to help the best he could. And he did. The detective knew he spoke to us. They spoke to each other. A lot was said. Frankly, more than I feel the need to share in this book. But there were two things that my mom's friend told us that stood out amongst everything else. Two things that were later to be confirmed. The first, is that the police were following my suspected attacker May 9, but were called away on a drug case. The second, was that the Police Chief was corrupt. That he attempted to make Boca Raton seem like it was a city free of crime. Free of anything or anyone that could shake people out of their sense of security. That could tarnish its pristine, perfectly manicured image. And I, with my previous history, was a perfect scapegoat. My story, and the crime committed against me, could get swept under the rug. I was stunned. Angry. Devastated. I believed him. In fact, it helped explain why I felt like I had to fight so hard to be taken seriously. But it also seemed like something out of a fiction novel. And I could understand if it seems that way to anyone reading this now. Thankfully, this dirty secret came out into the light. On December 8,1998, the Tampa Tribune[1] reported that U.S. Attorney General Janet Reno would open an informal inquiry to the Boca Raton Police Department for the practice of downgrading hundreds of crimes to enhance the city's safe image. The truth was out. I was happy it was. Not only for myself but for anyone else who was treated this way. And hopeful it would save others from the same fate. The second piece of information, that the police were following my suspected attacker, was reported about a year later.

The cover of the 2001 January/February edition of the Boca Raton Magazine[2] was simple. A mug shot of a man's face. A man named David M. The article, a true crime expose, detailed him as "A Predator Among Us." David was born in March 1954, and was described as a handsome man with *GQ* looks. He came from a wealthy family. Drove a Porsche. Belonged to country clubs. Had beautiful wives. But a sinister side lurked behind his good looks and fast cars. He had a police record that dated back to 1977. Assault. Battery. In 1980, he was arrested for sexual assault and spent four years in prison. While there, he apparently put on a good show for the attending counselor, who reported, "Resident does not appear to be criminally oriented. The instant offenses may be somewhat situational."

In 1986, he and his family were able to convince his first wife, a beautiful woman with a daughter from her previous marriage, the same. He was set up, they explained. And she believed them. After all, he had treated her and her daughter amazingly well. Three months into their marriage, however, the facade began to crumble. He admitted to having an affair, so she told him to move out. A few months later, he called the hair salon she was at and told her he had a gun and threatened to kill everyone there. It was disturbing, but she didn't think he was capable of murder. That is, until she received a knock on her door a few months later. A neighbor was at her door telling her to be careful. A little girl had been taken from her bed and stabbed in her backyard. It turned out that little girl was a friend of her daughter's. Other incidents occurred nearby. Assaults had been reported by a sixteen year old, as well as a thirty year old. The police didn't consider the incidents related. But she divorced him.

Two years later, David met and married a fashion model. They were married in 1989. While she was away, David was found with a six-year-old girl in his car. A six-year-old girl, a .38 caliber ladies' Smith & Wesson handgun, a knife, nunchucks, and rubber gloves. She had been taken from her bed in the middle of the night, but because she couldn't remember how she got there, he was spared from a nine-year prison sentence. He served three instead. And his second wife divorced him.

Upon his release in 1993, his wealth declined as well as his parents' health. Beginning in 1996, attacks on women near his home intensified. The magazine went on to describe five females, between the ages of 7 and 43, who were attacked in one year. And although there wasn't enough evidence to link him, police won't rule him out as a suspect. On January 7, 1997, he attacked a 24-year-old woman in the laundry room of her apartment complex. He started to strangle her with a tie. It broke, she started screaming, and he fled. She was able to give enough details for a composite drawing. By June, he attacked another woman in her home, stabbing her in the chest. The magazine went on to describe two more attacks, including one in an elevator in March 1998. Just as one of my nurses had described. The article reported that the police were frustrated and began following David M. But not on May 9th. Just like my mom's police friend had described. They weren't following him the night I was fondled and stabbed seven times in my bed.

Shortly thereafter, the magazine went on to describe that David M. met another woman who was married with a son. She described him as instantly falling in love with her and, by August, they went on their first official date and were engaged in 1999. The attacks, however, continued. Three more occurred by January 1999. The third woman died. She was found with a butcher knife in her back on her kitchen floor. The police were able to track her whereabouts, and a bartender was able to identify her. He also confirmed that David M., whom he knew by name, had danced with her the night before.

Because of this, the police felt they had enough evidence to name him as a suspect in the paper. This resulted in other women coming forward. Enough that could identify him in a lineup. A trial followed. He was sentenced for one of the victims. It was reported that his new fiancée told the victim to "Shut up" as she wept upon hearing the verdict. A second trial would be held. One that allowed two cases to be tried together. Both of which had identified David M. as their attacker. It was reported that David's fiancée tried to say he couldn't have attacked one of them, since they went to South Beach to celebrate their one month anniversary at the time. Thankfully, the jury saw through it. He was found guilty of two counts of attempted first-degree murder and two burglary charges. The sentence: two consecutive life terms to run consecutive to the 40-year sentence in the first case that had been tried separately.

I cried as I re-read this article. David M. was never convicted for my case. Or countless others. I wasn't able to identify him by his picture. I do remember telling the detective I could pick my attacker out of a lineup if I heard him speak. I felt confident about this. Especially if they made them repeat the words he said to me that night. "Don't worry, I'm a friend of your mother's." It still makes me cringe. But I was never given that chance. I don't know why. And I don't know if he'll ever be found guilty in my case. I used to be very angry about this. And it's still unfair. For both myself, and all of his victims. But I learned that letting those feelings fester would do me no good. I had to trust. Trust this was the man who attacked me. Trust he would stay in jail for the crimes he was convicted for. Trust that I could heal and move forward with my life, despite the fact he tried to end it.

I've cried more trying to type these words. I wanted to stop. I thought, *This is too much. I can't do this anymore. It's too hard.* But I couldn't. I couldn't stop writing. Not for myself. Not for the other women and children he's victimized. Brutally attacked. Traumatized. And in some cases, killed. I know my life will never be the same. I imagine they share similar feelings. I've never met any of his other victims, proven or suspected, but I believe we share an unspoken bond. One that unites us. One that unites us to all victims of violent attacks. And by victims, I mean survivors. For that is truly what we are. I hope that by sharing my story, I share understanding. Hope. Courage. Strength. Perseverance. And above all, to trust that each one of us has the power to consistently choose love over hate.

---

1. Tampa Bay Times, Dec 8,1998. Updated Sept 14, 2005. https://www.tampabay.com/archive/1998/12/03/reno-orders-inquiry-into-boca-raton-crime-stats/
2. Ocker, Lisa. "A Predator Among Us". *Boca Raton Magazine*. Vol. 21 No. 1. January/February 2001.

Chapter 15

Please just listen

Cause and effect. Right vs. wrong. Good vs. evil. These constructs have been in our consciousness for millennia and, at 21, I understood just how deeply rooted these concepts are. To say that I've never subscribed to them would certainly be untrue. But my mind is curious. And this curiosity allowed me to sift through the comments, reactions, and, at times, cruelty I faced when telling my story to unearth a profound, yet simple truth. The unknown is a frightening place to be.

Our minds yearn for comfort. Safety. Stability. They want to be wrapped in a cozy blanket, sipping hot chocolate in front of a fire. Soft embers dancing gently in the air, crackling with delight. Finding the cause for an event allows us to stay snuggled up in this comfy place, secure in our knowing. It's unfathomable to allow any other possibility. Especially so close to home. The earth beneath us would shake, shattering the foundation we believed was impenetrable. Our safe space torn asunder as we find ourselves falling into the abyss.

My story did just that. Many people insisted I must have known him. One such conversation went like this:

"You must have known him."

I respond simply, "No, I don't know him."

"Well, then, your mother must know him."

"No," I repeat, "this isn't someone we know."

They continue incredulously, "Then, how does he know where you live?"

"I only went to two places," I explain.

"The drug store I work at sometimes when I'm home and the mall. They're both close to her house, so he must have followed me from one of those places."

"And you don't think you would have noticed someone following you?" they retort.

"Not in such a short distance, no," I respond, wondering if I should have, in fact, noticed. Wishing desperately, I had. I continue with pieces of the story. Perhaps with the hope they will hear me. Understand me. See me.

"After I got home from the hospital, he called me on the phone." Their eyes grow big and bright, and their chest puffs up as they interrupt me. "See, he HAS to know you. How else would he have your phone number?"

I sense they feel as though they've caught me, that they've proudly exposed the truth. I don't back down.

"Our number is in the phone book and there are only

two Forney's listed in Boca Raton," I respond. "So it wouldn't be that hard to figure out which one was ours."

Still determined to prove their belief to be true, they ask, "Well, how does he know your name? That doesn't make any sense if he didn't already know you."

My body shifts as I feel the anger and frustration shoot up from the base of my spine. Each vertebra locking into position. My body finding itself, once again, shoved into this disparaging place. People insisting, arguing, demanding, that I *must* know him. Why can't anyone listen to me or believe me? I'm constantly heartbroken.

"Because every paper in South Florida, and I mean *every single one*, listed my full name, my age, my mother's name, our address, where I went to high school and where I go to College. THAT'S how he knows my name," I say in a firm tone.

Some people didn't want me near them. Certainly not in their homes. Especially not to spend the night. My mother was sometimes allowed once I left Boca to go stay with my dad, but not always. One couple opened their home to us, and I am forever grateful to them. I understood people were scared, but it was a terrible feeling just the same. To be shunned. Talked and speculated about. Doubted. Blamed. Felt sorry for from afar. Any kindness shown to me will forever live in my heart, but unfortunately, so will the cruelty.

I know that cruelty was not necessarily peoples' intention, but those reactions left a wound. Often, an uplifting gesture from some was met with harsh judgment from another. Reconfirming that people will claim they know some sort of "truth" since that keeps them out of discomfort. When I was still in the hospital, I remember talking to my mom about my room. She told me she had hired steam cleaners for the carpet, (that must have been a shock) but there was so much blood, they couldn't get it clean. I told my mom I didn't think I could walk into the same room, where everything had happened, and asked if there was anything she could do to change it. Obviously, the carpet had to be replaced, which meant everything had to come out. She said she understood. A group of beautiful souls came over one day and helped her repaint. A little girl left a dream catcher for me that still to this day hangs over my bed. When I got home, everything was different. New furniture, new paint. I was overjoyed. It didn't make it so that I could sleep comfortably in there, but I could at least be in that room. Additionally, a security company donated an alarm system, which was incredible for us both. So much generosity. Shortly after I got home, to a fresh room, and some hope, a good friend's mother said to me, "Don't you think that was a bit much, Lynn? I mean, to make your mom get new furniture and everything? Seems a bit extreme, don't you think?"

There were times it seemed just my presence made people uncomfortable, even if they were completely unaware of my story. I had a large arm bandage from my elbow down to my fingers, with just the tips peeking out. It literally looked like the bat that caveman Fred Flintstone waved around. I also had a white brace on my lower leg. I went to the grocery store one day, and this woman looked at me and loudly announced, with a bit of a sarcastic tone, "Woah, you better not hit me with that thing!"

"Don't worry, I won't," I awkwardly replied.

"You have to be careful walking around," she continued. "You're likely to knock everything over with that huge thing ha ha. Everybody look out!"

When I thought about returning to school in the fall, I knew it would be a struggle, but I really didn't know what to expect. I desperately wanted one thing, just one thing, to be a little easier. Parking on campus was an absolute nightmare. My arm brace had come off, but I would be in the one on my leg for a long time, probably about a year. I never allowed myself to believe this, but there was a definite possibility I would always have to wear it. I asked my orthopedic surgeon if I could get a temporary handicap placard. I only intended to use it on campus, because I knew there were people who needed it more than me. The brace rubbed my leg raw at times, so trying to get to and from campus on the bus and walking long distances was unappealing to say the least. He was very understanding and obliged. One day, I was wearing jeans, and as I was driving away, I could see in my rearview mirror a guy standing in the middle of the street, waggling his finger at me, and yelling, "You don't need that handicap sticker. You don't need that. No, you don't. You don't need that handicap sticker at all."

A roommate's mother also felt the need to lecture me,

after finding out what happened. "I really can't believe you went as far as to get a handicap sticker, though. Don't you think that's a bit ridiculous? I mean, there are people who really need those. Do you honestly think you're one of them?"

This last response, though short and to the point, spoke volumes to me. When I told an older gentleman that a man woke me up in my bed and stabbed me multiple times, he responded with this: "What did you do to piss him off?"

Over and over, I was left wondering why. Why did people react like this? What was the purpose? Had they not thought about what they were saying? I understand everyone is entitled to their opinion, but they were so quick to judge. To react. To shame. To blame. Why was that? And then it hit me. At twenty-one years old, I came to understand something so simple, yet so complicated. Cause and effect. If something so heinous could truly be random, it could happen to anyone. At any time. For no reason at all. And that feels unacceptable. Unsafe. Unbelievable. It is the foundation of victim shaming and blaming. They must have done something to bring that upon themselves, therefore I must have done something to bring this upon myself. My anger, though still there, also turned to compassion. Compassion for the vulnerability that my story made people feel. Compassion for their desperate need for this to somehow be my fault. Because this kept them from feeling vulnerable. Unsafe. And although I came to understand and accept this, I can tell you not much feels worse. It's horrible. And every time we desperately search for a cause, it often comes at the expense of the one who was victimized.

My response, after all this time, is hope. The hope that we can listen. Truly listen. And be vulnerable. Noticing not just their vulnerability, but also our own. It's uncomfortable, and difficult, but so much beauty could spring forth from this space. It could shift how we see each other. How we see ourselves. Allowing our minds to stay cozy by the fire as the unknown approaches, knowing the foundation will remain strong beneath us. All while sipping the proverbial hot chocolate as Louis Armstrong croons in the background- singing of green trees, red roses, and this beautiful, wonderful world.

Chapter 16

Returning to Life (the best I could)

After that phone call, the one where my (suspected) assailant asked why I started screaming over and over, I had to leave town. I just couldn't stay there anymore. I felt guilty for leaving my mom. I still kind of do. But, I also wondered if she might receive more support from friends after I left. That was certainly my hope. I had also felt strongly that I wanted to be close to my orthopedic surgeon. Thankfully, I still made many trips to see him over the next year. But, like I said, that phone call sent me packing.

My dad was living near Tampa at the time with his second wife. He flew down so that we could make the trip together in my little blue car. When we pulled out of the driveway, something kept tugging at me. I've found it difficult to ask for things throughout my life. I often felt like I was being a burden. But I couldn't ignore the strong desire

I had to go thank the people from the fire station. I asked my dad if we could stop there, and he, of course, said yes.

My dad and I walked in through the door of the fire station, and all of the men were quite welcoming. They were smiling and friendly, and I would imagine curious since I don't think they receive visits from strangers all that often. I started to tell them that I wanted to thank them for helping me. That I lived just across the street. They started describing someone else. Another girl who lived nearby, but on a different street. I said no. That wasn't me. They had helped me about three weeks ago. And I live literally "right over there". I turned and pointed towards my mom's house. When I turned back around, I was met with very different expressions than the ones I had been greeted with. I swear they all looked at me like I was a ghost. They seemed taken aback and a bit stunned. After a few moments, they regained their composure. We all talked for five, maybe ten minutes. They were kind and seemed happy that I came by. It made me feel happy to thank them.

I told my mom about the interaction. Later, she had something interesting to add. Her friend's ex husband worked as a firefighter in that exact station. He was off the night of my attack, but he obviously spoke to them about me. They apparently described me as, "the worst case they had ever seen. They couldn't believe I made it to the hospital alive, much less lived at all." It certainly explained their reaction upon realizing who I was. I'm not exactly sure how I felt when I heard it. I still have trouble.

It's kind of like hearing it about someone else. But it also makes me take note of my resiliency.

That summer was challenging to say the least. I was in physical therapy and occupational therapy. I had this wild new brace they had to build for my wrist, complete with fishing wire. I was also in a brace for my leg. But, despite everything I had been through, I never had any doubt I would return to school in the fall. When I think back to that now, it seems kind of crazy. But I did it. And would do it again.

I remember walking into my first class that semester with some of my fellow dancers. It was an academic class called Dance Appreciation taught by the Co-Chair of the Department. It became obvious to me that not everyone thought I would be back. I received a surprised, yet warm, reception. Many hugs. And a few tears. I don't think I could have prepared myself for how difficult it was going to be for me to watch my friends dance. Rehearse. Perform. Continue doing what I so desperately loved and wanted to do. I took a composition class (choreography) that fall because I knew I could still craft phrases and small solos with the brace on my leg. Thankfully, the one on my arm had been removed. But I would stay in the leg brace for almost a year. At first, I didn't take any technique classes. In the spring, I decided to take jazz. I would just have to do the best I could. It was awkward. Challenging. I felt like I had to get to know my body all over again. And it would feel that way for a long time.

Many tears were shed that first year. But I couldn't

imagine being anywhere else. I continued Physical Therapy on campus. I also found a therapist. Most days I knew I would get the brace off. That I would dance again. My wrist and my ankle/foot may not function exactly like they did before, but I would figure it out. I would just have to. I'll admit, however, there were times where that belief shattered all around me. I would fall into despair. And just sob. Wonder why this had happened to me while the "What-if's" suffocated me. What if I never dance again? What if I'm never going to be as good? What if I can't do it? But somehow, I always returned to my strength. My fortitude. My determination. Because I knew I would never give up. I wouldn't let myself. I refused to let it be an option.

In addition to the tears, I also had times of intense fear. I got home one day to find one of my roommates had left the back door open. And when I say open, I mean wide open. I was terrified. And angry. How could they have been so careless? I called a friend and begged her to stay on the phone with me. It was a two-story house, and my bedroom was on the second floor. It was dark up there and I had to get to the top of the stairs to turn on the light. (It was a very old house). I trembled as I glued my back to the wall and slowly climbed the stairs. Sideways so my back would stay touching the wall at all times. I got the light on. And checked the rooms upstairs. I was grateful that my caring concerned friend talked to me the whole way through. I can feel my body constrict as I share this. I was petrified. That particular moment was incredibly tense. There were others. There were also times I don't think I was aware of it. But I now understand there was always an underlying sense of terror within me. Always present in my body. And to some degree, there still is.

That undercurrent of terror was, and perhaps still is to a degree, pulsing through me. But something else courses through me as well. My strength. My resolve. And my determination to not let this event, this man, determine the outcome of my life. I fought with everything I had to live. And I would do just that.

In addition to my determination, I also felt supported and loved by my professors and friends. I had even started dating someone, a close friend of my brother's whom I had met a few years prior. I know they didn't always know how to approach me, or what to say, but I'm so grateful they always tried. One of the best gifts I was given came from my ballet professor, Isa. A fiery, petite, Cuban woman with one of the biggest hearts anyone could have. She was married to Ric, whom I also admired and adored. She choreographed a piece specifically for me. I would be in the spring concert. I would soon be onstage, performing again. I sat in a chair, wearing a dress with a gigantic skirt. A few dancers danced En Pointe around me, manipulating my skirt as I danced in the chair. My back and arms twisting, turning, exploring all of the space around me. My neck and head following their lead. Towards the end, the other dancers took the skirt, ran around me until they pulled it up off my body and ran off stage. I stood and came to the front. In my leg brace. Only able to do a tiny fraction of what I was able to do prior to May 9. As thankful and blessed as I felt to be performing, I couldn't help but feel ashamed and embarrassed. Worried that I would look terrible trying to dance in the leg brace. I was overwhelmed with joy, fear, shame, gratitude, and sadness all at once. My fears had led me to tell my new boyfriend not to come. I was worried he would think I was terrible. But at the last moment, I invited him. I'm thankful I did. He's now my husband and I'm so glad he was there to share this moment with me.

Back onstage, we had finished the piece. The other dancers came out for their bow. Then it was my turn. When I lifted my body back up, I was stunned. For a brief moment, I was frozen as I looked out into the audience of that beautiful large auditorium. People were clapping. Cheering. And standing. An overwhelming amount of people in the audience stood up for me. I was in awe. Tears welled up in my eyes. It felt nothing short of incredible. I was deeply touched.

Thank you, Isa, for creating that dance for me. The dance you lovingly named, "Lynn's Back."

Chapter 17

2014. Therapist's Office.

EMDR (Eye Movement Desensitization Therapy)

I was referred to this therapist specifically because of her expertise with trauma. I knew my past would be included in the work, but my main motivation was healing more deeply from the attack. She's an incredible therapist, certainly one of the best I've seen. And, although difficult, EMDR proved to be an incredibly powerful tool, revealing more than I could have imagined.

"This is making me nauseous," I say as my eyes follow her fingers back and forth.

"Okay," she responds. "Close your eyes. We can do this a different way." My eyelids fall, shutting out the contents of the room. I sit atop a soft couch. But rather than match its quality, my body remains tense. Rigid. Stiff. The whirling sensation in my stomach slows. Air methodically flows into my nostrils. Tap. Tap. Tap. Tap. Her hands lightly tap my knees. Quickly. Back and forth.

Back and forth. Air escapes out. Tap. Tap. Tap. Tap. My spine, despite all efforts, begins to soften.

"Imagine you're in a little boat," she gently says. "One that is taking you to the safest place in the world." And then I see it. Me. In a little rowboat. Gliding across smooth clear water. No effort is needed on my part. The gentle breeze knows just where to take me. My "safe place." One that is only for me. No one can get me here. I approach a house on a little island with huge glass walls. Walls that allow me to see everything around me. At all times. No surprises. The waves gently crash onto the beach. Seagulls squeal with delight in the distance as the sun's rays twinkle upon the water. My body relaxes here.

After some time in this glass house, it's time to leave to embark on the next part of this journey. I return to the boat. As I sit down, I gaze upon my safe place. I'm told I can return instantly any time I need. But for now, I must continue on. The breeze gently blows and the boat glides along the crystal water once more. In the distance, I see a cave. As I approach, I'm assured this cave is safe. Nothing can harm me. But it's important that I go. There's something inside I need to see. As my mind creates this vision, I'm aware of the room I'm in and how my body feels in it. It's as if I'm in two places at once. My pelvis and legs suddenly feel like lead. So heavy. Like a statue. Frozen. The rest of my body feels like a balloon. Floating. Billowing. Tethered to this statue that is my lower half. Despite these weird sensations, I stay with my vision. Cautiously, I step into the cave.

It's dimly lit. A bit wet. I'm not sure I like it here. But I continue on deeper. I learn that I'm here to see my younger, five-year-old self, and what she went through with the eight-year-old boy. As I continue to walk, I'm told there is a TV screen. One that will show me what I need to see. One that will allow me to see it, but not relive it. One that will keep me safe. I peer a bit further, and there it is. It's kind of small. Like a TV from the fifties. Suddenly, it turns on to reveal black and white fuzz bouncing all over the screen. Relief and frustration spill out from me. Relief because I don't want to see; frustration because I know I need to. I want to leave this shitty cave. But I chose to be here. I chose to take this journey. I want to face this pain that has been buried deep within me for so many years. I remain steadfast, determined to see this through. As I stare at the screen, the image starts to shift. It's out of focus, and I can't make any of it out. I keep staring. Back in the therapist's office, my legs are still lead, glued to the couch. But my torso suddenly shoots up to the sky and feels like it's one hundred feet tall. Like I drank the little bottle from Alice and Wonderland. I certainly feel like I'm in some version of that place, but it's a lot less fun.

These sensations, I'm assured, are okay, even though they feel weird as hell. Back in the cave, I keep trying to make out the images on the screen. I can't. I just can't. It's time to try a different approach. My brain is really trying to keep things locked away, far from my reach. Attempting to circumvent this, my therapist takes me on a different path. Some twists and turns later, I come to a forest with tall trees. I see some movement not too far from where I stand. As I look closer, I see her. Peeking out from behind a tree. Timid. Shy. Lonely. She is wearing a cheerleading outfit. One that I've seen pictures of myself in. One that I wore when I was four and cheered for my brother's little league team. It's tattered and torn. Covered in dirt. Sticks and dead leaves are matted in her hair and clinging to her clothes. In her hand is a little white stuffed bunny. One that I used to carry everywhere with me. "I still have that bunny," I softly tell my therapist. I look at this little girl. I assure her it's okay, but as I do, I'm overcome with sadness. She's been stuck out here, scared and alone, for so long. How could this have happened?

I have to earn her trust. Slowly and gently, I do. I need her to open up to me while understanding I'm here to help. With her guidance, I begin to go through the experience I had with the neighbor boy. But this doesn't seem to be her story. She's about a year younger than the girl who had that experience. Something else is here. I'm confused. It doesn't seem quite real. Am I making this up? Is my brain trying to create a falsehood to explain this pain I've been carrying my whole life? This pain that I could never truly understand? As I'm contemplating this with my therapist, and trying to make sense of what's happening, I realize we've been transported. This little girl and me. No longer are we in a forest. Now, we're in a room. A room with a small table placed in the middle. Suddenly, the little girl is lying on the table. As I realize this, I'm overcome with a strange sensation. My body transforms into a smokey mist, quickly pushing up and spreading across the ceiling. All that is left of me are my eyes. Two big eyes that float in the middle of this mist, up on the ceiling. Looking down at this young girl laying across the table.

She's clean now, wearing the same cheerleading outfit from before. But now it looks new. Tan with a big C on the chest. She's awake. Her eyes are open, but she's not really moving. In fact, she seems frozen. Terrified. As I look down on her, I sense another presence is here in the room with us. A shadow. It approaches her. As it does, it becomes more solid. A man. But one that remains in shadow form. His eyes glow yellow. His fingers like claws. He stands over her. Stares at her with a Cheshire grin. Suddenly, the images become hazy. Disjointed. I can't see clearly anymore. I try. I desperately try. I think I have a sense of it. But I'm confused. Lost. Angry that I got disconnected. Desperate to help the little girl. Desperate to help me.

I pleaded with my therapist. Was this real? Why couldn't I see it clearly? "Sometimes, that's all we're able to see when we've completely dissociated during an event," she explained. " Especially when we're so young."

During subsequent sessions, we revisited this. I was able to see a bit more, but the scenario was similar each time. She assured me it had happened like this for others. How they would see their abuse play out. Many looked down from the ceiling like I did, some even describing it the same way. A mist with eyes. In her experience, everyone questioned if it was real. If they were recalling something that they had seen on TV, or something that actually happened to them. That it took a while for the truth to sink in. To accept.

Even now, because my memory is still limited and disjointed at best, it's easy to still question what happened. To wonder. To ask if this really happened. But I know. Somewhere, deep down, I've always known. I was sexually molested as a young child.

My Mistress

When thoughts of you dance across my mind,
My face softens, my lips gently smile,
Anticipating the comfort and peace you'll bring,
Like you always have since I was a child.

When I sense the tips of darkness appear,
I can feel it yearning for me,
Its tentacles slither, loop, and twirl
Gliding up and around my body.

As it threatens to take hold over me,
In the distance you appear,
Your sweet, soft, familiar glow,
Is something I hold so dear.

I'm in awe of your power to slay the dark beast,
You've never failed before,
Your presence still excites me,
And always leaves me wanting more.

You are an intoxicating enchantress,
Lighting my way in the night,
And once I bring you to my lips,
Everything just feels right.

My mind quiets, my heart breathes,
And for a moment I find peace,
You are my oldest, truest friend,
I long for this feeling to never cease.

The tranquility of this moment,
Bathes over every cell of me,
But deep down, I know what is to come,
For now, I can finally see.

I feel how quickly I lose control,
The pure serenity so short lived,
I thought you were here to comfort me,
To take my sins away, to forgive.

But now I know what lurks inside,
Your beauty a ruthless disguise,
Your power does not chase the darkness away,
You are my true demise.

Your claws sink deep into my skin,
Your fangs drip with desire,
To keep me locked in this cage,
In solitude, controlled by your ire.

Your possession of me is transparent,
My foolishness now also known,
Falling for your slick deception,
Blind to the depths of your cruel soul.

I must find the courage to escape you,
To forgive myself for calling you friend,
I needed comfort and companionship,
And, my heart, you promised to mend.

I will find a way to escape your grasp,
The truth is unearthed, the path revealed,
You will not continue to enslave me,
My fate is my own, it is not sealed.

I break the bond that was created long ago,
I take back the freedom you stole,
I forsake you and all you are,
I reject you, and on my own, am whole.

Chapter 18

Present Day

"I want the cookies!" Says my inner child, often.

One month ago, on the morning after Halloween, I was walking in my neighborhood. My eyes gazed over to the right to a sidewalk that led to a house. My eyes followed the white cement, up to the porch, and there, perched perfectly at the edge, was a pile of candy. For a moment, I was frozen mid stride. Staring. Giddy. My eyes twinkled with delight as I took in the sparkles and glitter that danced around the pile of goodies. My inner child was suddenly riding a unicorn. Holding a magic wand. Giggling with glee. Exclaiming, to all in her kingdom, "Free candy!"

Free candy, indeed. But not anything I needed. Or probably really wanted. I have come to understand that no food is good or bad by nature. But at this point in my life, I do know that sugar (ie My Mistress) is something I still struggle with. I use it, and at times, abuse it to mask my feelings. Or avoid them. Or to "fill me up with love" when I feel sad or lonely. I know logically that sugar will do none of these things. It wasn't the chocolate I was really after. It was the excitement. The glee. The feelings I had when I saw that free pile of goodies. And I think my inner child felt the same.

Breathing in this insight, my adult, grown-up self, turned away from the candy and continued walking. I wasn't consciously aware at that moment the exact conversation that took place between my adult and inner child. But, upon reflection, I do know one took place. And not because I resisted the urge to run up and snatch all the candy. But because I remained calm. Content. Satisfied. Not bitter or angry that I "never get to have any fun" or "get what I want." Something I could have easily felt in the past. And, if I'm being honest, sometimes still do. The difference between this moment, and ones where I want to stomp my feet with indignation, was my willingness to have that conversation with her. To See her. Hear her. Love her.

I believe the conversation would have gone something like this:

Adult: "If no one took that candy, it's probably gross. And you'll likely get a tummy ache if you eat it."

Child: "But I want it. It's candy. It might be stuff I like. You don't know."

Adult: "Doubtful. It's been there all night. It won't taste very good."

Child: "I could just sneak up there and check. No one's looking. It's free candy!"

Adult: "I know it seems fun. But I'm pretty sure it's going to make you feel awful since it's been sitting outside all night. Tell you what. If you still want candy later, I have a car. I have money. We can go and get candy that you'll actually enjoy. Something you really want. I promise."

Child: Rides away on her unicorn waving her magic wand. Secure in knowing I'll keep my promise if she really wants it.

Amazingly, she never wanted any candy. At least not that day. I think just making her feel seen, and validating her desires, was enough. I can understand how she felt incredibly lonely and isolated in the past. And at times, still does. In her desperation to be seen, heard, and loved, she acts out. She doesn't know how to process these huge, overwhelming emotions that fill her small body. So much sadness. So much anger. So much grief. For years, she screamed at the top of her lungs for help. All cries fell on deaf ears. I didn't know how to listen. Or how to love her. But I'm learning.

I think it's easy to forget about our inner child. Or, in some cases, accept we even have one. Generally, we are taught very young to "grow up". Stop being "childish". To leave behind our youthful fantasies. Some children do, in fact, grow up quickly because of various circumstances at home. Some survive unimaginable horrific circumstances. And some children grow up in what seems to be a perfect home. No matter what, however, one thing is certain. We all have a wounded child that lives within us. A wounded child that needs your attention. Your patience. Your love.

If it seems I'm leading you into the territory of "blame your parents for everything", I assure you, I'm not. Although some healing may need to take place regarding your upbringing, I encourage you to take full responsibility for your wounded inner child. Perhaps you avoid them. Or you're angry you have one. Or you deny one is even there. But I invite you to look. To listen. To meet them. I think you'll find that they've been trying to communicate with you for a very long time. This task isn't necessarily easy. But it could change your life. If you're thinking that this concept is weird or absurd, I invite you again to consider it. Or, if you're like me and your favorite method is avoidance, I encourage you to step fully into this task.

There are a number of ways to meet your inner child. I've tried many. Hypnotherapy and NLP are great ways. EFT Tapping is another. Here, I'll offer this. (And if you know tapping, you can certainly do that at the same time.) Close your eyes and imagine yourself as a child. Really focus. Allow whatever age that feels right to emerge. When you have a clear picture in your mind, imagine sitting across from them. Take a moment to really look at them with curiosity and wonder. They may look at you with the same. Or they may seem shy. Or sad. Or angry. Rather than trying to control them, allow them to fully be themselves. Tell them they are welcome here. That you love them. And that you are here to listen. And do just that. Listen. Openly. Patiently. No one is going to tell them their feelings aren't valid here. No one is going to shame them for who they are or how they feel. No one is going to hurt them ever again. Because you are here to protect them. To love them. To cherish them.

Once they communicate their needs and feelings with you, tell them that you will always be here for them. Any time they need you. Plan to visit them often. Even if it's just a quick check-in. What sounds like fun to them? What color do they want to wear? What do they need? You may be surprised by the answers, You may be even more surprised how this can shift your perspective. Your attitude. The way you see yourself. And more importantly, how you treat yourself.

If we treated ourselves with more kindness, how would that shift how we treat others? What might change in the world if we recognized everyone's wounded inner child? What if the next time you sat across from someone, you saw just that? What would change in your perspective? Especially those that seem to trigger you? I certainly encourage anyone to speak up for themselves when needed, but would it allow you to come from a less reactive place? I don't want to imply that this will solve the world's problems. Nor do I believe in "spiritual bypassing". It takes work. It takes looking at yourself honestly and being brave enough to enact change. Change is scary to our primal "lizard" brain. It sees it as a threat to our survival. Because it often was. But today, we can choose to see it differently. Just like we can choose to see others differently. Instead of reacting blindly the next time your blood starts to boil, is it possible to ask yourself why? Why you're reacting, getting angry, etc.? Can you take a few breaths the next time you find yourself losing control, and observe? I'm aware this is no small task. And perhaps it won't always be possible in the moment. But, if you're willing to consider another perspective, you'll likely find you don't have all of the information. We assume a lot. Is it possible to ask your inner child how they felt at that moment? Did it remind them of another time they felt that way? And what would be true for the other person or people involved?

So often, we approach life from our wounded inner child. Because we vehemently try to avoid the feelings and situations that wounded them in the first place. But what if they could find solace? Peace? Joy? How could that change you? Change others? Change the world? Perhaps there would be a little less hatred, and a lot more glitter, magic wands, and unicorns.

Chapter 19

She just looked at me, with tears in her eyes, and said, "Thank you."

March 2019

Backstage, covered in sweat, I quickly changed into my next costume. A red dress with a form fitting bodice, tight sheer sleeves, and a skirt that spreads wide when I spin. I was so happy when I found it. I had ordered one on Amazon, but it made me feel frumpy and sad. I refused to do that to myself. I had been stuck in too many costumes throughout my life that didn't flatter me. This was my choreography. My solo. My story. And I would do it justice. I searched for ballroom dresses, thinking that might give me the fit and flare I desired. And, I was right. There it was. Simple. Elegant. Beautiful. It was so close to what I had envisioned. It was more money than I wanted to spend, but I ordered it anyway. Once it arrived, I pulled it out of the box, and put it on. I looked in the mirror and did a spin. As it caught the air, it fluttered and flowed around me. I knew this was the one. This was the dress that would make me feel beautiful as I kicked, twirled, and leaped across the stage. The one that I would take off and abandon the last quarter of the dance. The one that would draw me back in towards the very end. The one I would pick up as I stood alone, under a red spotlight. And, as the lights began to fade, the one I would use to strangle myself.

Standing offstage, I heard the audience clap, signaling the last number was finished. The dancers pant as they ran past me, and I stepped onto the dark stage. My stomach fluttered as I found my starting position. I inhaled and steadied myself for what was about to happen. I lifted my arms, crossed my right foot over my left, and exhaled. Suddenly, lights illuminated the stage as fast driving violins flooded the air. And, alone, in my beautiful red dress, I danced my heart out. Spilling forth all that's inside of me.

My choreography has always come from a deeply personal place. One that allows me to transmute my feelings. My emotions. The thoughts I'm unsure how else to express. It comes naturally to me. I feel at home on the stage. Safe. Powerful. Free. For me, there's nothing else like performing. And when I perform my own work, those feelings are amplified. They vibrate through every cell of my body. And it is my greatest desire that those vibrations travel out into the audience. Buzzing and swirling around them until they move through them. As those vibrations dance inside their bodies, they wake something up. Feelings and emotions that have been stuck. Ignored. Dismissed. Or perhaps it offers a different perspective. Physically seeing before them emotions they have had trouble understanding. Expressing. Comprehending. And, although they may not understand how or why, it allows those emotions to flow through them. To be released. To be freed.

That particular show I was performing remains special in my heart. Six dancers came together, with great vulnerability and strength, to expose some very personal truths. We spent a lot of time in the process. First exposing ourselves more deeply to each other. Then to the audience. The theme of the show centered around things we, as a society, generally don't talk about. We were also asked to research our theme and share our findings with each other. I created a group piece about loneliness. As the lights faded up, a silhouette of four dancers would appear. Each inside their own box. I called it Brink. And it made me cry when I saw it unfold before me. I'm so thankful those dancers trusted me to create that piece. I know it wasn't easy. And, although I feel like I brought something special with that dance, I also had something else inside that I needed to say. Needed to express. I had trouble figuring out exactly what it was, but I knew this was the time. For years, I had envisioned myself dancing in a red dress. I saw myself take it off, too. (And, yes, I had a short unitard underneath. Also red.) I thought it might end up being another piece about the relationship I have with my body. I still struggle. And I hope one day I can find peace with it. But this work, I discovered, would be about something entirely different.

I got into the studio, still unclear about the story behind the work. But I needed to start as our show was quickly approaching. Generally, I see things play out in my head before I start moving. If you were a fly on the wall in one of my rehearsals, you would see me just stand there and stare off into space. A lot. I also use other tools, such as improv, but I'm extremely visual. I didn't know the exact movements, but I had a clear outline in my head. I also knew the style of music I wanted with it. I started to play around with movements, still thinking that this might center around eating disorders or body dysmorphia. And suddenly, mid movement, it hit me. I knew exactly what this piece needed to be about. Post Traumatic Stress Disorder. PTSD.

In all of my therapy, I had never talked too much about that specifically. I got startled easily, and I discovered I disassociated more than I realized. Not to the extent of becoming a different personality, but, as my trauma therapist explained, I remained in a constant state of it. It made it hard for me to be fully present in my body. And I know that sounds incredibly strange for someone who has spent their life using their body to express themselves. In a way, I feel like dancing was the only time I really felt connected to my body. Otherwise, it was easy to slip out. I would experience it a few different ways. I often lost short periods of time. No more than a few seconds. I remember one time, in dance class oddly enough, I was on the side of the studio waiting for my turn to travel across the floor. A few moments went by, and my friend started to talk to me, and I kind of shook my head a bit and laughed, "I'm back." I had no idea where I went. But in those few seconds, a fire could have erupted in front of my face and I would have had no idea. I had basically blacked out. That happened often, whether I felt anxious or not. Other times my head would feel like it was a huge balloon. Either a hot air balloon, still attached to my neck, or a smaller helium balloon attached to my neck by a long thin string. I also experience the sensation of floating. This would happen often in bed. I would feel like I was about three feet above my body. If this all sounds strange, it is. But it was pretty normal for me. The trauma therapist helped me so much with this. I feel those sensations far less. In fact, most days not at all. I am still kind of jumpy, though. For instance, I still let out a sound and jump a bit off the ground if my husband comes into a room when I'm not expecting him to. Even when I know he's home. This was happening often leading up to this show. But nothing prepared me for what happened that day driving to dance class and rehearsal.

I was on a one way street. And I see there are people around on the sidewalks, looking at men in the middle of the street. Two men were on top of a third and they were punching each other. They were bloody. And focused on each other. I stopped in front of them and started wondering what to do. Do I call the police? Get out and try to stop it? Why is no one else intervening? Does that mean I shouldn't? Then my brain switched to escape plans. I can't back up because someone is behind me. Can my car jump this curb? I'm not sure because it's so low to the ground. And there are people around. Do they have weapons? Guns? Am I about to get shot at? As my mind raced, they stopped and looked up at me. All three of them, still hiding their positions. Then, the men standing backed up and got on one side of the street. The other stood up and moved to the other. And I just drove. I started feeling guilty. Should I have helped? Should I still call the police? I felt terrible. And a little shaken.

I walked into the studio and someone asked if I was okay. I started to explain what happened and what I should do about it. The response seemed to be sympathetic, but not overly concerned. It was unfortunate, but probably best to stay out of it. And they went on with what they were doing. I, however, felt tears start to stream down my face. My stomach felt shaky. The danger was over. I was safe. So why was I getting more upset? I even thought about the possibility I did help in some way. After all, the fight did break up. But it didn't help. As I looked around, I started crying even more. I told my friend (also the Artistic Director) I didn't know why I was so upset and started apologizing. I was embarrassed. She told me to take all the time I needed. I thanked her, apologized again, and headed to the bathroom. My whole body was shaking now as I cried harder. Why couldn't I get a hold of myself? I was confused, frustrated, ashamed. I put my back up into the corner of the stall and slid to the floor. My tears turned to audible sobs. The small shakiness I felt turned into violent tremors. I couldn't control anything in my body. Yet, I was completely aware mentally of everything around me. I knew I was safe. I knew I wasn't in any danger. I could hear the music playing from the dance class I was missing. And couldn't help but think that everyone must be wondering what the hell was wrong with me. But I couldn't stop. For over an hour. I sobbed and shook for more than an hour on the floor of the public bathroom. It was humiliating. Terrifying. Confusing.

My heart hurts for others who have experiences like this. It hurts more when I read articles about PTSD. And when I read that people trigger others on purpose, I was livid. I couldn't believe it. PTSD survivors were tormented because others' thought it was funny. A joke. Not real. I was angry. And instead of sitting in anger, allowing it to seep in and take me down, I wanted to transmute it. Transform it. It made me more determined. More brave. I realized it was not only my story I was sharing. It would be from my perspective, of course, but it was for anyone who could relate. Anyone who needed to be seen. Conversely, it was also for anyone who couldn't relate. Who needed *to* see. And I would use my beautiful red dress to help me show them.

On stage, I smiled in my lovely dress and performed movements that would indicate I was powerful, happy, and free. Then suddenly a red light would shine that would stop me in my tracks. Just how PTSD did to me. It appeared out of nowhere, grabbed hold, and set me free when *it* decided to. Only then could I regain my composure. I mirrored this feeling in the dance. Once this sequence happened three times, I ran back and forth, pleading for help until I threw myself to the ground. At this point, I shook and writhed, pulling at my dress. Then I had to get it off of me. This dress that once made me feel so beautiful. I moved away from the dress feeling more exposed. Moving more disjointed. Then I couldn't help but be pulled back to it. I slowly picked it up and held it along the front of my body. I began dancing again. Balancé, balancé en tournant with my partner. I was hopeful in those brief moments. Then, slowly, contemptuously, the red spotlight illuminated the stage, setting its sights on me. I grabbed the sleeves of my dress, wrapped them around my neck, and began to strangle myself. Just as PTSD strangles those it possesses.

After our performance, we held a Q & A. From the audience, a young male told me he cried during my performance. Something in it allowed him to open up and weep. I didn't fully know what to say, but I could feel my heart expand.

Privately, a close friend came up to me after the show and just said, "Lynn.....your solo....your solo."

Another private moment was shared with a different woman. A woman I didn't know. She stood in front of me with her hand over her heart. Her eyes welled up with tears, and she said, almost in a whisper, "Thank you.

Thank you." Tears formed in my eyes as we just looked at each other.

This is why I created that piece. The one that exhausted me both physically, mentally, and emotionally. The one that also helped me heal. The one I entitled, "**P**lease Know **T**riggers **S**eldom **D**iscriminate."

Betty

A tiny spark lay in the distance,
One so fragile and new,
Lay dormant like a seedling,
Just bursting to break through.

It sends out a signal,
Searching the globe,
Wondering which special person,
Can decipher its code.

Wondering, waiting,
"I can't wait to be found,"
But as the time ticks away,
The spark sinks deeper in the ground.

The joy drains away,
"I'll never find my mate,
The one I am meant for,
The one to change my fate."

Its hope fades away,
Its light grows dim,
"I may as well succumb,
I have no choice but to give in."

As the spark descends,
With sorrow and grief,
Its course rapidly changes,
And is left in disbelief.

"Who just rescued me?
I thought for sure I was dead!"
And the spark gazes upwards,
To find you instead.

"It is you, my mate,
We were meant to be,
I am an idea,
And it is you who'll set me free."

Joy floods your body,
As you embrace your new friend,
For you, too, had felt empty,
Your heart needing to mend.

"This is it," you exclaim,
"This will make me whole,
I will proceed forth, with glee,
It will be something to behold."

As you and your spark
Form this new partnership,
Your mind races with wonder,
It even does a backflip.

You smile and you skip
Your heart dances with delight,
You can't wait to bring this idea
Out into the light.

As your mind opens up
To what's possible and new
You notice another voice,
That's now here with you.

It is quiet at first,
But quickly explains
"I will be heard,
I will stake my claim."

Your chest grows heavy,
You let out a sigh,
For this is no stranger,
Whose come in the night.

This voice has been with you,
For many years it seems,
It always shows up,
And ruins your dreams.

It makes you feel small,
Worthless, and dumb,
This voice, you know,
Is difficult to overcome.

It tells you, "You'll fail,
Why bother, just quit,
You know you'll lose,
You are an idiot."

"Not again, not again
Why do you do this to me?
Why are you so hellbent
On making me unhappy?"

"Every time I try
To achieve something new,
You come smash my dreams,
Make me feel so blue."

You turn to your spark,
"I'm sorry my friend,
I'm no good, I'm defeated,
I won't win in the end."

The spark looks at you,
And sees your pain,
But it vibrates and states,
"A new perspective you'll gain."

"Give this voice a name,
And a personality, too,
Ask it some questions,
Why is it part of your crew?"

You ponder this request,
Wondering what this will do,
But you shrug, "Why not,
I'll try something new."

This, my friends,
May seem weird, untrue,
But if I can do it,
Well, so can you.

I'll explain to you now,
How it happened for me,
So that perhaps one day,
You can try it and see.

Eyes closed, I breathed,
Asked this voice it's name,
"Betty," she replied,
With a hint of disdain.

I allowed this voice, Betty,
to come into view,
Leather catsuit, red lips,
And a whip to boot.

She stared me down,
Harsh look on her face,
Ready to berate me again,
And do so with haste.

I mustered the courage,
Looked her straight in the eye,
"Dominatrix Betty,
You're so terrible. Why?"

"It's so blatantly obvious,"
She strongly replied,
"You're safe with me,
I keep you alive."

"Remember the first time,
You felt embarrassed and shamed?
Well, I showed up after,
Swore we'd never feel that again."

I was shocked at first,
I couldn't believe my ears,
But I softened as I realized,
She tried to keep me safe all these years.

I looked at her,
My view fresh and new,
And said, "I thank you, Betty,
I really do."

"But from now on,
I've got it from here,
I can keep us all safe,
Please trust me, dear."

I sensed her reluctance,
To completely let go,
But she had to take a back seat,
Though we needn't be foes.

I told my new spark,
"Come here, sit by me,
The road may be bumpy,
But I'll finally be free."

"Free to explore,
seek, and discover,
New roads ahead,
All full with wonder."

I turn to you now,
Inviting you, too,
Discover the voice,
Deep inside of you.

The one that's mean,
Degrading, and cruel,
Ask them their name,
Why they do what they do.

You all have your own Betty,
I know that you do,
Face them now,
And speak to them true.

Politely, with love,
tell them to step back,
Explain, "I've got this,
And that's a fact."

"I need you to trust me,
I really do,
Cause plain and simple,
we've got some shit to do."

Chapter 20

Present Day

I'm a Fraud

I struggled with the point of this book. Why should I write it? Why is this important? I want to help people with my story, but how? Who am I to try and help others? And how can I be authentic when I'm ashamed of the times I didn't make the best choices? Deep down, there's a core truth that I desperately want to hide. Bury. Pretend doesn't exist. To put it bluntly, I'm scared. I'm scared to be found out. Found out that I'm a fraud.

I was recently offered a job and I was told why they liked me. I don't think the particulars are very important, but the reasons they liked me were not what I was expecting. Nor what I wanted to hear. I would be an addition to the team, and the person proceeded to tell me over the phone: "Well, *obviously,* you're very different from (the person currently employed). I mean, she's *young, fit,* and just *full of energy*. I don't know how she has so much energy.....I think you'll *really* appeal to older people."

What. The. Actual. Fuck.

I was shocked. Devastated. Confused. And just felt like a huge worthless pile of shit. If I was *obviously* so different from young, fit, and full of energy, that could (in my mind) really only mean one thing. I was old, fat, and lazy. Which, my brain (ie Betty) told me, also meant ugly. And stupid. I felt so stupid. Because, ultimately, it *wasn't* obvious to me. I didn't feel that I was so different from the other employee. In fact, I questioned if I would get this job because we might be too similar. I was a little older and a little bigger, sure. But I would compare our differences to a small pond. A cute pond. One with lily pads gently floating on the serene water. Peacefully. Until a few tadpoles begin to playfully wriggle at the surface. And underneath the bright blue sky, butterflies and dragonflies dance among the flowers in the morning dew. Apparently, however, our differences are much more vast. Much greater. Much more obvious. Instead, they are the size of the Atlantic Ocean. In a storm. Dark turbulent waters thrashing underneath an ominous sky. Thunder angrily rolling across gray, jagged clouds. Sailors doing their best to traverse these treacherous conditions. Their hopes high, until horrible, wretched sea hags lure them to their deaths.

I've struggled with my self-esteem my whole life. If I didn't achieve something I wanted, a perfect grade, a dancing or acting role, an award, I immediately thought it was because I was too fat. Too ugly. Too stupid. And even as I write this, I notice the paradox. If I felt those things about myself, then why shouldn't others? But that's not what I wanted obviously. I wanted other people to notice me. Tell me I was pretty. To applaud my efforts. To tell me how excellent my work was. Not because I'm self centered or conceited. Far from it. I was desperate for validation. If others could recognize me for my work, my intelligence, my looks, then perhaps I wasn't a complete waste. And although I was desperate for it, it made me incredibly uncomfortable.

I remember in eighth grade my Spanish teacher looked at my school photo and said, "You know, other girls in this school model and I think you could do something like that."

Words formed in the pit of my stomach, and came hurling out before I could stop them.

"Oh, shut up," spilled out of my mouth. I was mortified. I had just told my teacher to "shut up." I quickly tried to retract my statement, stumbling around my words, apologizing profusely, while adding I couldn't do something like that. It still makes me cringe to this day.

Other times I received compliments, I would quickly shut them down. Tell them that's not true. I'm not those things that they were saying. I did this for years. Although I was ravenous for kind words, taking them in made my stomach convulse into knots. I was so caught up in my own feelings, and not wanting to come across as "full of myself", I never considered what my reaction was doing.

What I was really saying to the other person. I never recognized that, through my overwhelming need to be validated, I was completely invalidating them. I remember the day this truly set in. I was standing in the gym talking to one of my Pilates clients and her friend. They were saying nice things about me, but I stood there denying every word. No one seemed upset. In fact we were all laughing. But when I walked away from that conversation, it just kind of hit me. I thought, "Damn..... I'm an asshole. That must have made them feel like crap. I stood there and told them they were wrong and (although I didn't say this) stupid for thinking those things about me. Fuck." I'm not sure why it struck me so profoundly that day. I'm sure I had heard that before. But for whatever reason, at that moment, I got it.

In times past, this profound realization would have flooded my body with shame. Regret. And proof. Proof that I was, in fact, as awful as I believed. And that voice inside my head, one of my "shadows", would quickly appear. The one that reveled in my shame, and would gleefully reinforce all of the ways this was true. She would say, "See. You *are* a terrible person. You make other people feel like shit. Because you're stupid. Worthless. Undeserving." I had heard her so many times. Loud and clear. Demanding I bow to her every whim. And I often did. But in this moment, this glorious triumphant moment, I was in charge. I made her sit in the corner and shut her mouth. I was in control now. I had the power. The power of choice.

I made two important decisions that day. The first was not to listen to that hateful voice. The second, was to actively change my behavior. I would accept compliments graciously. It would just be that simple. Although I may not always feel the same, or be able to see what they were seeing, they didn't need to hear the ramblings of my insecurities. To have my issues dumped all over them. I would simply say, "thank you." Now, I'm not suggesting you keep all of your feelings bottled up inside. I can't stress how important it is to find people, whether close friends or professionals, who can support you. Help you. And offer tools to guide you. But I also believe that our words, our reactions, hold a lot of power. Not only for ourselves, but for others. Our energy has a direct impact on those around us whether we are aware of it or not. And I want my energy to be a positive one. I certainly don't succeed every time. Far from it. And those close to me often know how I'm really feeling. But I know that, no matter what, I ultimately have a choice. I have the choice to become an active observer of my thought patterns. My beliefs. When the train they're on speeds up and starts to lose control, I can become the conductor once more and ask myself, "Is this really true? Do I have all of the information I need to come to this conclusion? To make it a fact? Or are there other possibilities I'm not considering?" If I'm unable to regain control, I have the choice to seek help. To ask for advice, or an outside perspective, when I have less power over that insidious voice. That shadow part of myself. And I have the choice to realize that sometimes it's just not that complicated. Sometimes, I can simply choose to say, "Thank you."

Now, this may not seem obvious at first, but all of this relates to my recent experience around this new job opportunity. I've done so much work. So much therapy. I've come so far. So why did this comment make me completely fall apart? Sobbing alone in the bathroom for an hour. Here I am, trying to write this book, and I can't handle this? The woman on the phone didn't technically call me "old, fat, and lazy" but my brain sure did. Or more specifically, my shadow did. She happily appeared to feed me the adjectives that I secretly (and perhaps openly at times) use to describe myself. I didn't realize, however, just how deeply I believed them. When I told my coach, she offered this to me: "There's something here for you. Something to recognize. To learn from. To grow. A chance to see your beliefs reflected back to you. And a chance to love yourself more."

I'll admit, I'm pretty sure upon hearing this I did a huge eye roll. I was upset. It sucked. And I imagined a lot of other people would have a similar reaction as I did. Which, admittedly, justified my feelings a bit more. But when my ego settled, and my anger and sadness dissipated just enough to think a bit more clearly, I realized she was right. Like in the gym that day, I was given an opportunity. An opportunity to make a choice and then act according to my decision. I could let these words, and more importantly my reaction to them, ruin me. Expose me as a fraud. Prove I have nothing to offer anyone. And, therefore, it would only make sense to stop writing this book. Or, I could let these words empower me. Figure out where I was still coming up short. Where I wasn't showing myself enough kindness. Enough grace. Enough love. I can face those things head on. Examine them. And do the work. And while I do, I can still continue writing this book. Because I do have something to offer. And so do you. If you choose it.

Chapter 21

E-Talk

"Enough talk." This is a quote from the movie, Conan the Barbarian. Conan, played by Arnold Schwarzenegger, is confronted by his foes and they demand that he turns over the princess. He states, "Enough talk," and proceeds to take out his enemies. I've personally never seen this movie in its entirety, but my husband and his friends would joke a lot about that line. It was often used when they played video games together. When the time came to take action. And when the words "Enough talk" proved to take too much time, the quote was shortened: E-talk. It was spoken in a dramatic fashion, followed by laughter.

I tried to be annoyed with them, giving my best eye roll. But I couldn't help but laugh along with them. And even adopt the phrase myself. It didn't take long for E-talk to become synonymous with more than just video games.

It often became our own battle cry. When it was time to stop saying, "I want to" or "I wish I could." When it was time to simply take action. Enough talk. E-talk.

This phrase could be used for goals both small and large. There's something so decisive about it. Simple. To the point. No nonsense. Time to stop making excuses. I understand everyone has their own rhythm. Their own timing. And I encourage that. But I also think that the vast majority of us are great at making excuses. And when any amount of fear or insecurity is involved, those excuses become bigger. The list of reasons we "shouldn't" or "can't" grows longer. And that's when E-talk can step in and push you (gently or swiftly) into action.

The mere idea of taking action can seem scary to our brains. Our minds. Particularly, our subconscious minds. Scientists now estimate that the vast majority of our decisions, actions, emotions, and behaviors depend on brain activity that lies beyond our conscious awareness. In fact, up to 95% of it. The subconscious mind is quite powerful. It also stores deep beliefs and fears that develop during our very young, formative years. That's why I think mindset work is an incredible tool for all of us. The more we become aware of our thought patterns, deep seated beliefs, and fears, the more we can overcome them. This might sound a little strange, but you can talk to your mind like a well meaning, but overprotective friend. When you get an idea to try something new, for instance, you might be excited at first. Then, your mind will start to rattle off all of the reasons you shouldn't do it. All of the things that could go wrong. That it would be better to stay comfortable. Stick with what's known and familiar. Because, ultimately, that will keep you safe.

When beginning this process of "talking with your mind", it's important to notice these thoughts. Acknowledge them. And then acknowledge yourself for becoming aware of them in the first place. This step is hugely important, and it begins to break the pattern that has become deeply rooted in your brain. Second, you can try responding. Something like, "I hear you. I understand you're worried and scared and I acknowledge that this feels a bit uncomfortable. And I want to thank you for looking out for us both. I want you to know I've got this. I can handle it. I promise I will make sure both of us stay safe." Taking this a step further, you can then envision all of the good things that can come out of this new venture. Rather, *will*. Fun, excitement, a new career, a new love, discovering a new talent, etc. And more importantly, how it will *feel* once those things have come true.

In addition, our minds want to prove our initial thought (or belief) to be true. Let's go back to the example of trying something new. What beliefs do you notice coming up? Common themes might be, "I won't be any good", "I'll fail", or, "I'll get laughed at." Once you've had those thoughts, your brain goes to work to prove them to be true. It will recall the time you were made fun of, or had your feelings hurt. When you tried something, got frustrated, and gave up. When you were misunderstood or didn't feel supported. All of these scenarios give your brain enough evidence to "prove" your initial thoughts (ie "I won't be any good") to be true. Therefore, your brain will reason, you should quit now to avoid those same feelings, outcomes, etc. Once again, this is a pattern to keep you safe. And it's quite effective. But it can also keep you stuck and miserable. The truth is, you don't know the outcome. And, although that in and of itself might be a bit scary, what is on the other side could bring you incredible joy and fulfillment. But you'll never know if you aren't willing to try.

I may be sounding a bit like Pollyanna (again, referencing back to one of my favorite Disney films. The one where she plays "The Glad Game"), but I completely understand this isn't easy. It takes work. But my desire is to encourage you to try. To be bold. Brave. To "E-talk yourself."

My story, since early childhood, is filled with countless times I felt like no one heard me. No one listened. Where my power was stripped from me. It affected me for a very long time. And still does. But I also came to realize that I fixated on the times I silenced myself. And there are many. Then I would berate myself for it. I had to make a choice. I had to step up and realize there is a different way. And, it also makes me realize there are times when I did speak up for myself. I did take charge. I took ownership. I have had to train my brain to notice those times in my life. To accept those to be true, just as much as the other. And of that I am capable. No one is going to advocate for you as much as yourself. And I can't encourage you enough to do it.

Fight for yourself. Speak up. Whether it's for your physical health, emotional health, or anything else. I don't, however, think that means it's acceptable to be controlling or cruel towards anyone else. I believe the words "please" and "thank you" go a long way and I try to say them as much as possible. But I don't think you have to accept being dismissed. Or mistreated.

I also advocate for getting the help and support you need by the right people. One such example for me has been finding the right medications to help me. Four years ago, I experienced another bad bout of depression. My husband basically told me I needed to get help. I listened. Although I definitely have a defiant streak, I didn't take his comment in any other way but love. I found a wonderful Psychiatrist. After talking with her for 25 minutes or so, she asked, "Has anyone brought up the possibility of ADHD to you?"

I looked at her, rather wide eyed and intrigued, and said, "No."

In all of these years, no one had ever suggested that. But it makes so much sense now. And medication for it has definitely helped me. She also brought up that we could run a genetic test to determine which drugs worked best for my body. I was excited. It greatly reduced the guessing game. Once the test came back, it determined that my body didn't respond well to SSRI's (selective serotonin reuptake inhibitors). The only prescription treatment I had ever been offered for my depression. SNRI's (serotonin-norepinephrine reuptake inhibitors), showed they were well suited for my body. I'm not exaggerating when I say I could feel the difference in three days. I will not, nor can not, guarantee that this will be anyone else's experience. But this made such a positive impact in my life I would be remiss not to mention it here.

I feel it is also incredibly important to realize that, although medications can be incredibly helpful, and for some of us, necessary, they are only one piece of the puzzle. Mindset work is crucial. And, as I told my friend, medications allow you to implement the work you do more successfully. I'm a huge advocate of therapy. There are also numerous modalities that I've tried that have been extremely helpful. I've mentioned EFT tapping. I've also tried shadow work, hypnotherapy, NLP, breath work, various forms of meditation, and joined coaching groups centered around mindset and manifestation. They can all be extremely beneficial. I think the key is finding someone qualified, someone you trust, and being open to the experience. If you don't jive with the first person you find, look elsewhere. Doing any form of mindset work is challenging. It is a lot of work. it's not always pleasant, and takes a lot of courage. But it is so, so worth it.

One of the groups I worked with led me to a vocal coach. I have been interested in singing lessons for a very long time. But I rarely allowed it to be more than a passing thought. As I've shared, using my voice has often proven difficult. Especially given my history. But I would find myself thinking about it more after her workshop. For a year, I got the intuitive message to contact her. I finally listened and signed up for private vocal lessons. A singing teacher who also majored in Creative Writing and ran a coaching program. Amazingly, and totally unexpectedly, it led me here. Now. Sharing my story. And I can't thank her enough.

I am, indeed, immensely grateful. But this process was also hard. Really fucking hard. Mentally, emotionally, and even physically. When I would start to tell people in the past my story, I would end up saying something like, "My story is so crazy. I should just write a book."

I said this for years. Many years in fact. And somewhere, deep down, I meant it. But I was never really sure I would *actually* do it. I mean, where would I even start? How would I do it? What would I say? Why should I do it? Who *am* I to think I should write a book in the first place? It was scary. I was fearful. I still am. But in a way, the times where I cast my fear aside and did something anyway have been the most rewarding. I didn't know where those things would take me, exactly, but I suppose that was also kind of the point.

I can think back to times in my life where I purposely decided to do something that I was scared of. I *chose* to take action. I started to take acting classes in my early 30s. In college, I had to take an acting class as part of my dance major. I ended up liking it and thought perhaps I would like to continue. It took me ten years to follow through. It was uncomfortable. Kind of scary. And for a while, I knew

I was holding myself back in class. Then one day, I said, "E-talk." I knew I was only hurting myself by not putting myself fully out there. Now, I have an agent. I am a working actor. It's true I would love more auditions, more bookings, but the fact is I'm doing it. Like most actors, we get rejected more often than not. I'm certainly thankful for the projects I've booked, but I've often felt frustrated because I want to do more. So, I chose to take action. I wrote, directed, and produced one short film. One that I wrote knowing I would also be the lead actor. Now, I have written my second. A horror musical comedy that I will direct, produce, and act in, very soon. And I couldn't be more excited about it. Now, I could choose to succumb to the fears, the worries, that it won't be any good. No one will like it. I'll be laughed at. I could choose to wallow in the feelings of not getting enough opportunities, I'm not good enough, etc. etc. And, if I'm honest, sometimes I do. But ultimately, I know I have to make a different choice. One where I believe in myself. Believe in my work. And do what needs to be done to make it great.

I've continued to dance, choreograph, and perform my whole life. Because it's a huge part of me. I could have given up when I was stabbed. But I *chose* to make it work. I had always wanted to live in New York City. Ever since I attended the school of Alvin Ailey for their summer workshop when I was 17 years old. It turned out my life would not lead me there to live. And admittedly, it still makes me sad. But, in my 30s, I decided if I wasn't meant to be there full time, I would spend a month there. Over the summer. I would just try as many classes as I could. I was excited. And scared. That summer, I never fell asleep before 4am. Because I was alone. In a strange apartment. I had a feeling I might have issues feeling unsafe, but I didn't know exactly what to expect. Regardless, I refused to let that stand in my way. I faced it. I "E-talked" myself. And I did it. And it was an amazing trip. So amazing, I did it three more times.

With the pandemic, I hadn't danced in approximately two years. A long time for anyone, but especially someone in their 40s. But, I have missed it terribly. Plus, I have an idea for a dance on film I want to create. But I know I won't create it without being in better shape. So, I needed to go back. Not just for my body, but for my soul. But I knew it would be difficult. Clumsy. And embarrassing. And I started to dread it. And procrastinate. Why? Because my brain sensed my fear.

Betty came back to let me know how much I had screwed up.

"You should have been working harder."

"You're fat and out of shape."

"You're going to look like a fool," etc. etc.

But, I kindly told Betty to step aside. I made a promise to myself that I would attend by a certain date. No matter what. E-talk baby. And, even though those thoughts creeped in, I showed up. I kept my promise to myself. I did it. And, although it was tough, in the end, I know I'm tougher.

I believe we are all tougher than our fears. Tougher

than our inner critics. Tougher than our past. But it is up to each one of us to make that choice. To choose to find help when we need it. To choose to become an observer to our own thoughts. Our own actions. To choose to heal ourselves. Each other. To choose to break the pattern of abuse. Victimization. Cruelty. To choose to listen to our intuition. And, above all else, to actively choose love. The world can be so painful. So ugly. But it is also incredibly beautiful. You just have to choose to see it, even if it means a bit of E-talk.

The End

Chapter 22

Questions I invite you to ponder

I also invite you to try multiple ways to answer. Journaling, discussion, coloring, painting, voice to text, movement, vocalization.

Let's Talk about Fear

1. Think of a time in your life when you've been fearful or scared. I'm not necessarily referring to a life threatening situation, but rather a time when fear came into your consciousness and caused you to pause. It could be anything. Heights, public speaking, touching an insect, trying a new skill, starting a new business venture....you get the idea. Try to name a few. Then consider the following:

A. Times when fear kept you from doing something you had the desire to do. How did that make you feel? What thoughts/feelings came up for you? How does that make you feel now? What was the outcome? What did you take away from that experience?

B. Times when you pushed through the fear and did it anyway. How did that make you feel? What thoughts/feelings came up for you? How does that make you feel now? What was the outcome? What did you take away from that experience?

Is Fear Still Holding You Back?

2. Is there something in your life you would like to accomplish now? Is fear holding you back? How can you push through it? What resources/help/support could you find now? It may be helpful to imagine a scenario with little to no risk (touching an insect for instance). Then move on to "bigger things" that feel more risky.

A. Imagine not following through. How does that make you feel?

B. Imagine completing the task. How does that make you feel?

C. Imagine failing. What could happen? Is fear making everything seem bigger and scarier than it really would be? Sit in the feelings for a while. At the end of the day, take some time to reflect. How was your mood for most of the day? How did you make use of your time? What can you take away from this experience?

D. Imagine succeeding. What could happen? How do you feel when you picture a positive outcome? Sit in that feeling for a while. What do you notice? At the end of the day, take some time to reflect. Did anything shift for you? Were you in a better mood? Get more accomplished? What can you take away from this experience?

How You Can Heal

3. There are multiple healing modalities mentioned throughout this book. Which ones have you heard of? Which ones are new to you?

A. Have you tried any? What was the outcome?

B. In regards to ones you hadn't heard of before, do any of them sound interesting to you? Are you willing to try them? If not, why? What's really holding you back?

Leave Shame Behind

4. Victim shaming is prevalent, both in this book, and in our world. I ask the following with no judgment. We're all human. Reflect on times in your life when you may have

judged someone, not believed them, or been convinced you would have handled something differently.

A. Why do you think you had that reaction?

B. What influenced you when that happened? Other people? The news? Social Media? The need to feel safe?

C. Do you truly believe you had all of the information you needed to come to that conclusion? That belief?

D. What other possible conclusions or outcomes could you consider? How could that change your perspective?

Being a Good Caretaker for Yourself

5. How can you become a better observer of your thoughts? Your patterning?

A. Do you need some downtime? If so, be honest and take it.

B. Are you making excuses? Avoiding? Deflecting? How can you E-talk yourself?

6. It's important for your brain to know you can be trusted. You've got this.

A. How can you establish patterns of trust? When you say to yourself you're going to do something, actually following through. Start with very small goals. One example: Say to yourself, in your mind or even out loud, "I'm going to do the dishes today." Then, no matter what, do them. Once you've completed the task, take notice. Celebrate. You said you were going to complete a task, and you followed through. You did it. Notice how that makes you feel.

B. Notice if you can stay with the celebration. Or does the inner critic want to tell you, "It's not a big deal. It was just the dishes. You didn't do anything special", etc. Are you able to notice that self-talk? Are you able to tell it, with love, "Actually, it *is* a big deal. I made a commitment and I followed through. And that's worth celebrating."

It may seem silly, but the more you're able to do this with everyday, smaller tasks, the more it will translate into bigger, scarier things you would like to do in life.

7. How can you be more curious? What might you discover? Can your inner child help you with this? How would they investigate and navigate through the world? What can you learn from them?

8. What scares you? How can you step boldly forward and do it anyway?

* * *

Take that leap.
Get out of your own way.
You'll never know what it's like to fly
if you never try!

Resources for Support

National Alliance on Mental Illness (NAMI)

- 800-950-NAMI (800-950-6264) or text "NAMI" to 741741
- nami.org

Anxiety and Depression Association of America (ADAA)

- adaa.org

National Institute of Mental Health (NIMH)

- nimh.nih.gov

* * *

American Psychological Association

- apa.org

American Psychiatric Association

- psychiatry.org

It Gets Better Project

- Itgetsbetter.org

RAINN (Rape, Abuse & Incest National Network)

- Rainn.org

National Center for Victims of Crime

- victimsofcrime.org

Victims Support Services

- victimsupportservices.org

Acknowledgments

Carissa Lynn Renner: Vocal coach to writing coach and everything in between. I'm so incredibly grateful that I found you. You gently guided me to use my voice, boldly and authentically, and encouraged me when I needed it most. Thank you from the bottom of my heart.

To my fellow Sirens in Carissa's coaching program: Thank you for giving me the support, encouragement, and space to begin this journey. I have no doubt our time together was integral to the creation of this book. Thank you.

Joanna Baron (Aletheia Program): Thank you for your guidance and encouragement.

Lindsey Lekhraj (The Designer Genes Co.): Thank you for all of your support and motivation.

Sophia (Artistic Director of Artivism Dance Theatre) and my fellow dancers who created "The Elephants" and "Our Unmentionables": I truly believe we created something special. Thank you for sharing that process with me.

Linda Naef: I've had many wonderful therapists along the way, but my time with you was potent and life changing. I'm forever grateful.

Dr. Jessica Clark Chandamuri, Psychiatrist: You helped me immensely.

To my dance professors at the University of Florida: Ric, Isa, Joan, Rusti, and Kelly. I love you all so very much.

To Dan and Jane and my entire Boca Ballet family: thank you.

To my friends who loved and supported me during that time in my life: I love you more than I can say. It will always mean the world to me.

To anyone who visited me in the hospital, called, or sent cards or well wishes: Your kindness will always be cherished. Thank you.

To my mom: You are a strong woman and I love you.

To my dad: I love you and I miss you so very much. (Especially your sense of humor and gift of storytelling.)

To my brother: I miss you. And I love you.

To those who are close to me now, I know I can be a handful! Thank you for loving me.

To anyone reading this book, thank you.

About Lynn

Lynn Forney loves bold bright colors, being silly, hugs, and honey mustard. She feels most at home performing on stage and loves delving into anything that allows her to express her creativity.

She currently lives in Austin, TX with her husband and their two rescue dogs.

You can reach Lynn at:

- **www.lynnforney.com**
- **choosingsurvival@gmail.com**

Can You Help Me?

Would you help someone you had never met? What if you could help them in a meaningful way without it costing you a cent?

If your answer was, "Yes!" then I have an opportunity for you!

Would you be willing to help me share my story with the world?

My ask is simple.

People do judge books by the cover and reviews are a form of social proof that your book is worth a reader's time and investment. I want to share my story with the world and that will require a village of willing helpers!

One of the most helpful things you can do to help an author out is to **review their book on a book-**

seller's platform. Let other readers know what you loved and learned!

If you feel so inclined, posting a picture of yourself with the book, or the cover of the book on social media with your honest review is also helpful.

Together, we can do great things! Thanks in advance for your support!

Made in the USA
Middletown, DE
02 October 2022

11539326R00096